A Handbook for Enhancing English-Medium Program Quality and Practice:

Towards Effective Teaching, Learning and Assessment

Authored and Edited by
Beverley A. Yamamoto and Don Bysouth

Osaka University Press
Osaka, Japan

Copyright © Beverley A. Yamamoto and Don Bysouth 2015
Published by Osaka University Press, Osaka University, 2-7 Yamadaoka Suita-shi, Osaka, Japan 565-0871

Printed in Japan
ISBN 978-4-87259-502-4 C3037

All rights reserved. No part of this publication may be reproduced or transmitted in any form or by any means, electronic or mechanical, including photocopy, recording, or information storage and retrieval systems, without permission in writing from the publisher.

Contents

Notes on editors and contributors ⋯⋯⋯⋯⋯⋯⋯⋯⋯⋯⋯⋯⋯⋯⋯⋯⋯⋯⋯ iii
Acknowledgements ⋯⋯⋯⋯⋯⋯⋯⋯⋯⋯⋯⋯⋯⋯⋯⋯⋯⋯⋯⋯⋯⋯⋯⋯⋯⋯ v

1. Introduction – A User's Guide ⋯⋯⋯⋯⋯⋯⋯⋯⋯⋯⋯⋯⋯ 1
                         Beverley A. Yamamoto and Don Bysouth
    Setting the Context for the Handbook ⋯⋯⋯⋯⋯⋯⋯⋯⋯⋯⋯⋯⋯ 1
    Creating the Scaffolding for Quality Enhancement ⋯⋯⋯⋯⋯⋯ 3
    The Global 30 Project and Paying Attention to Outcomes ⋯⋯⋯ 4
    Visualizing 'Quality' Practice ⋯⋯⋯⋯⋯⋯⋯⋯⋯⋯⋯⋯⋯⋯⋯⋯⋯ 7
    The Purpose of this Handbook ⋯⋯⋯⋯⋯⋯⋯⋯⋯⋯⋯⋯⋯⋯⋯⋯⋯ 9
    Navigating the Handbook ⋯⋯⋯⋯⋯⋯⋯⋯⋯⋯⋯⋯⋯⋯⋯⋯⋯⋯⋯ 11

Part One   Creating the Framework for Enhancing the Quality of English-Medium Programs and Courses
                         Beverley A. Yamamoto and Don Bysouth

2. Scaffolding Quality – Key Curriculum Concepts ⋯⋯⋯⋯ 17
    Benchmarking ⋯⋯⋯⋯⋯⋯⋯⋯⋯⋯⋯⋯⋯⋯⋯⋯⋯⋯⋯⋯⋯⋯⋯⋯ 17
    Learning Outcomes ⋯⋯⋯⋯⋯⋯⋯⋯⋯⋯⋯⋯⋯⋯⋯⋯⋯⋯⋯⋯⋯⋯ 20
    Curriculum Alignment ⋯⋯⋯⋯⋯⋯⋯⋯⋯⋯⋯⋯⋯⋯⋯⋯⋯⋯⋯⋯ 23
    Syllabus Writing ⋯⋯⋯⋯⋯⋯⋯⋯⋯⋯⋯⋯⋯⋯⋯⋯⋯⋯⋯⋯⋯⋯⋯ 25
    Course Learning Outcomes ⋯⋯⋯⋯⋯⋯⋯⋯⋯⋯⋯⋯⋯⋯⋯⋯⋯⋯ 28

3. Levels of Learning and Instructional Methods ⋯⋯⋯⋯⋯ 43
    Levels of Learning ⋯⋯⋯⋯⋯⋯⋯⋯⋯⋯⋯⋯⋯⋯⋯⋯⋯⋯⋯⋯⋯⋯ 43
    Instructional Methods ⋯⋯⋯⋯⋯⋯⋯⋯⋯⋯⋯⋯⋯⋯⋯⋯⋯⋯⋯⋯ 45
    Selecting Instructional Methods ⋯⋯⋯⋯⋯⋯⋯⋯⋯⋯⋯⋯⋯⋯⋯⋯ 54

4. Assessment as Linked-up Practice ⋯⋯⋯⋯⋯⋯⋯⋯⋯⋯⋯⋯ 59
    Forms of Assessment ⋯⋯⋯⋯⋯⋯⋯⋯⋯⋯⋯⋯⋯⋯⋯⋯⋯⋯⋯⋯⋯ 60
    Assessment Methods ⋯⋯⋯⋯⋯⋯⋯⋯⋯⋯⋯⋯⋯⋯⋯⋯⋯⋯⋯⋯⋯ 61
    Selecting Assessment Strategies ⋯⋯⋯⋯⋯⋯⋯⋯⋯⋯⋯⋯⋯⋯⋯⋯ 67
    Using Criteria and Descriptors ⋯⋯⋯⋯⋯⋯⋯⋯⋯⋯⋯⋯⋯⋯⋯⋯ 72
    Preventing Plagiarism and Setting Internationalization Goals ⋯ 74

5. Feedback as Practice in Dialogue ⋯⋯⋯⋯⋯⋯⋯⋯⋯⋯⋯⋯ 77
   Student and Instructor Feedback ⋯⋯⋯⋯⋯⋯⋯⋯⋯⋯⋯ 77
   Samples of Assessment Types with Instructions
   and Associated Feedback and Criteria ⋯⋯⋯⋯⋯⋯⋯⋯⋯ 81

6. Moderation - Ensuring the Reliability and Validity
   of Assessment ⋯⋯⋯⋯⋯⋯⋯⋯⋯⋯⋯⋯⋯⋯⋯⋯⋯⋯⋯⋯⋯⋯ 105
   Internal Moderation ⋯⋯⋯⋯⋯⋯⋯⋯⋯⋯⋯⋯⋯⋯⋯⋯⋯⋯ 106
   External Moderation ⋯⋯⋯⋯⋯⋯⋯⋯⋯⋯⋯⋯⋯⋯⋯⋯⋯⋯ 109
   Course Leader Reports ⋯⋯⋯⋯⋯⋯⋯⋯⋯⋯⋯⋯⋯⋯⋯⋯⋯ 109

Part Two Reflections on Teaching and Learning on an English-medium Program

7. Introduction – Teaching Reflections ⋯⋯⋯⋯⋯⋯⋯⋯⋯⋯ 127
   Viktoriya Kim, Saori Yasumoto and Christie Lam

8. Syllabus Design ⋯⋯⋯⋯⋯⋯⋯⋯⋯⋯⋯⋯⋯⋯⋯⋯⋯⋯⋯⋯ 131
   Viktoriya Kim

9. Assessment Issues in Multicultural Classrooms ⋯⋯⋯⋯ 139
   Saori Yasumoto

10. Management Issues in Multicultural Classrooms ⋯⋯⋯ 145
    Christie Lam

11. Enhancing the Role of Teaching Assistants
    in the Delivery of English-medium Courses ⋯⋯⋯⋯⋯⋯ 153
    Yukiko Ishikura

Part Three – From Handbook to Practice
Beverley A. Yamamoto and Don Bysouth

12. Conclusion – Enhancing Quality and Practice ⋯⋯⋯⋯⋯ 161

Notes on editors and contributors

The editors and main authors

Beverley A. Yamamoto is Director of the Human Sciences International Undergraduate Degree Program, School of Human Sciences, Osaka University. She has been overall responsible for the delivery of the program, working particularly on curriculum design, development and quality assurance. She is also Professor of Education, Gender and Sexuality Studies in the Graduate School of Human Sciences. Beverley has taught and contributed to program development in both UK and Japanese universities over the past 20+ years. Her research interests include the internationalization of education and health promotion in educational settings, especially sexual health.

Don Bysouth is an Associate Professor in the Graduate School of Human Sciences, Osaka University. Trained as a social psychologist, Don has worked at universities in Australia, the United Kingdom, and Japan, and since 2009 has been involved in program and curriculum design, and quality assurance and enhancement initiatives for the Human Sciences International Undergraduate Degree Program (where he heads the Global Citizenship Major). His current research involves interactional analyses of teaching and learning practices employed in a range of higher education internationalization contexts, with a particular focus on cross-cultural practices in COIL and ICT based settings.

Guest contributors

Christie Lam is an Associate Professor in the Human Sciences International Undergraduate Degree Program, Osaka University. Before joining the G30 program in 2011, she taught sociocultural anthropology in universities in Hong Kong and Australia. As a core team member of G30 program (Global Citizenship Major) she has contributed to curriculum development and implementation of a range of interdisciplinary and anthropology related courses.

Saori Yasumoto is an Assistant Professor in the Human Sciences International Undergraduate Degree Program, Osaka University. Saori has taught in universities in Japan and the United States. Her current research explores issues in gerontology and the sociology of family.

Viktoriya Kim is an Assistant Professor in the Human Sciences International Undergraduate Degree Program, Osaka University. Viktoriya holds a PhD from Osaka University. Her recent research focuses on international marriage and an investigation of the implementation of the International Baccalaureate program in Japan.

Yukiko Ishikura is a doctoral student in the Graduate School of Human Sciences, Osaka University. Over the past three years, she has been involved with the Human Sciences International Undergraduate Degree Program from two different perspectives: as a Teaching Assistant and as a doctoral student researching English-medium programs. Her research interests lie in the field of internationalization of higher education, program assessment and development, and student teaching and learning.

Acknowledgements

The editors would like to thank all those who have contributed directly or indirectly to the production of this Handbook. We are especially grateful to our guest contributors who offer their personal reflections on their own practice as instructors and as a teaching assistant on the English-medium degree program that has been the springboard both for this and for earlier in-house editions of this Handbook.

A special word of thanks is due to Ms Yoshiko Furuya who helped first secure the grant that enabled the production of this publication, and then waved carrots and cracked whips, as necessary, to ensure that we met deadlines.

We would particularly like to thank two previous directors of the Human Sciences International Undergraduate Degree Program, Professor Yasumasa Hirasawa and Professor Masayuki Nakamichi who offered words of support and expertise every step of the way as we put into practice over the past four years many of the ideas contained in this Handbook. We would also like to thank Professor Kiyoshi Higashijima for understanding the value and importance of the Handbook to the quality of our program.

It goes without saying that the students on the Human Sciences International Undergraduate Degree Program deserve special thanks for being patient with us when we did not get things quite right, for being honest but gentle with feedback and suggestions, and for believing from the beginning that it was possible to offer a high quality, full undergraduate degree program in English in a Japanese national university.

Finally we would like to thank our respective family members for putting up with us while we panicked over deadlines and tucked ourselves away in our rooms to finish the final draft over the holiday period.

Beverley Yamamoto
Don Bysouth
2 January, 2015

One

Introduction
– A User's Guide

Beverley A. Yamamoto and Don Bysouth

Setting the Context for the Handbook

This Handbook can be viewed as both a precursor to and product of the Global 30 Human Sciences International Undergraduate Degree Program that we designed in 2009-2010 and have offered for the past four years at Osaka University. In other words, it can be framed as both an input and output of this English-medium degree program. It brings together the theory and practice that has guided us over the past four-plus years as we have endeavoured to create a teaching and learning quality assurance culture. We have put together our ideas and experiences into this Handbook in the hope that it will also play a role in supporting the endeavours of other program providers and instructors seeking to deliver high quality English-medium programs.

    We feel that the ideas contained in this Handbook are essential to the enhancement of program quality, and teaching and learning practice. We have to confess that none of the ideas and suggestions here, are on their own, particularly new. We have synthesized both theory and good practice here, and added a heavy dose of hands-on experience, to produce a guide that may assist those who are setting out to launch English-medium programs or those who are interested in teaching and learning quality enhancement, particularly in institutions where another language is the primary medium of instruction. We visualize the ideas contained here as scaffolding supporting the delivery of high quality, individual English-medium courses that come together to create a high quality degree program. It is scaffolding that should support innovation and not smoother it.

When asked to develop an undergraduate English-medium program in the Human Sciences as part of the Global 30 (G30) project in 2009, I (Beverley) was aware that to provide a program that would not only reach an internationally accepted minimum standard – a quality threshold – but also transcend this would require that everyone involved worked together mindful of what kind of graduates we wanted to nurture. It would require that all involved were working for the same broadly defined teaching and learning goals. This would, in my mind, require a level of dialogue about teaching and learning practices, and learning outcomes, possibly rarely seen in Japanese universities. It would also require this to be an on-going dialogue aimed at continuous quality enhancement. Given our highly pressured lives and the multifaceted roles that we as academics have to perform, I was also keenly aware that the program had to be built on sustainable practices that would not cause burn out after the first year.

I (Beverley) received my academic training in the UK and was involved in the designing and delivery of two Master's programs by a blended pedagogy of distance learning and more traditional face-to-face teaching and learning over a period of sixteen years at the University of Sheffield. This meant that I had my own teaching quality scaffolding to draw on. Yet from the beginning, I realized that I could not just import UK teaching quality practices and expect them to work at Osaka University, even if the teaching and research base were not dissimilar. I knew I would have to work with colleagues to create something that would maintain the best practices of the Japanese system and the strategies that sustain these, while also working towards a quality threshold that would ultimately satisfy the highly qualified, mobile students we expected to join our program.

After being charged with designing and delivering the G30 Human Sciences Program I immersed myself in the relevant research literature on teaching and learning, quality assurance as well as English-medium instruction (EMI). I supplemented this knowledge-base by visiting Higher Education Institutions (HEIs) in the UK to talk about professional development (PD)[1], program design and quality assurance strategies.

Don joined the program in November 2009 and brought with him knowledge and experience from working in Australian and UK universities. He was keen to work with me on quality assurance and there began a partnership that lead directly to this Handbook.

---

1) We are aware that in Japan the term Faculty Development (FD) is more commonly used, but we have chosen to use the more generic term Professional Development (PD) in this Handbook.

Creating the Scaffolding for Quality Enhancement

From the beginning we were aware that the key challenge, but also potential strength of our program, would be the diverse backgrounds of key stakeholders. We could not assume common understandings to ensure we were all on the same page. Not only did we expect to be working with a diverse student body, but also with instructors from diverse backgrounds. The future instructors of our G30 undergraduate program were likely to range in experience from entry level academics to full professors. Not only this, it was also highly likely that they would have grown up in a variety of cultural and educational contexts, and be teaching from a number of Human Science disciplinary perspectives. Our program is an interdisciplinary, international program. Knowing that we could not assume common ground among students or course instructors, or between students and instructors, it was clear from the start that providing a clear and easily understood framework to bring us together, so that we could deliver a coherent program, was always going to be a high priority task.

From the curriculum design stage we started to draw ideas together to create a Teaching Quality Handbook that could be used in PD practices. After Don joined the program we were able to work together to produce an in-house publication, *The Osaka University Teaching Quality Handbook: A Guide to Best Practices in the Provision of Teaching and Assessment for Undergraduate Degree Programs*, which we made available to instructors on the G30 program in 2010 in English and Japanese. These Handbooks, English and Japanese editions, were then used for PD work both for the G30 program and more widely in Osaka University.

While only in-house publications, we soon had frequent requests for copies of the Handbooks from program providers or instructors working in other HEIs in Japan and beyond, as well as from Heads and Deputy Heads of secondary schools. This led to a greatly expanded Second Edition, which we produced in 2013. With the scope of English-medium programs and course delivery expanding in Japan and other parts of Asia, this book edition of the Handbook is our response to a growing number of requests to make the contents of the original in-house publications more generally available. This Osaka University Press version has been further expanded with an eye to speak to practitioners beyond our university and beyond even Japan.

We are particularly pleased to have been able to add to this book version of the Handbook reflections on teaching and learning practice from our four guest contributors, who have been delivering the Human Sciences International

Undergraduate Degree Program for between three and four years (Christie Lam, Saori Yasumoto and Viktoriya Kim) or supported the program as a Teaching Assistant on numerous courses as well as taking the program as a case study for her doctoral research on EMI in Japanese HEIs (Yukiko Ishikura). The Handbook is greatly enriched as a result of their reflections on implementing the quality enhancement strategies outlined in Part One of this Handbook.

One further development that is reflected in the additional material is the opening up of many of our course offerings to students on regular Japanese language programs and short-term exchange students. From the spring semester of 2012, we began to open up some of the courses to those students we have come to refer to as Non-G30 students. This study population is made up of regular Japanese students on main stream programs who have been educated within the context of the national curriculum and have little overseas experience; Japanese students educated partially overseas, but on regular Japanese programs; international students on regular Japanese programs; or short-term exchange students on the English-medium Osaka University Short-term Exchange Program (OUSSEP). While most of these students are undergraduates, the participation of graduate students is also notable in our classes.

This opening up of courses adds many challenges to instructors and to the task of quality assurance, but it also greatly enriches the learning environment and pushes forward internationalization. The teaching reflections in Part Two in particular address some of the issues raised by the combined G30 Non-G30 classes (classes with students on our HUS international undergraduate program and those from regular or short-term exchange programs) as well as some practical ways of addressing these.

The Global 30 Project and Paying Attention to Outcomes

The Global30 Project (G30), launched in academic year 2009-2010, was part of the government's ambitious plan to increase the number of international students from just over 100,000 to 300,000 by 2020. The G30 Project sought to enhance internationalization in the country's leading universities by supporting the development of English-medium undergraduate programs. Osaka University was one of the 13 universities awarded this generous funding in the first round. Due to a change in government and along with it a shift in educational priorities, there was never a second round of recruitment so to the very end the G30 universities numbered only 13 rather than the expected 30. Nevertheless, we have all continued to refer to this project informally as the G30 Project.

It was clear from the beginning that G30 was going to act as a pebble that was going to make rather large waves (Yamamoto, Ishikura and Bysouth, 2012). It would be impossible to deliver an undergraduate program without internationalizing procedures at every level (Knight, 2008) and ensuring that quality assurance strategies were in place. The focus of our activities has been in **internal quality assurance**. The strategies and practices outlined in detail in this Handbook are ones that ensure that 'a culture of quality is created, defined, supported and promulgated'[2]. They aim towards a continuous cycle of teaching quality enhancement.

When we began to plan the HUS program, we knew we would need to deliver a degree program made-up of 124 credits, with one course generally worth two credits. Language classes would be worth just one credit. When designing the program, we had to meet requirements regards not only providing a range of disciplinary-related courses at entry to advanced levels, but also a general liberal arts education in the first three semesters that included, sports and health, and second language requirements. Unlike many exchange programs that put together a stimulating general program by getting different schools and faculties to provide some of the contents, a full undergraduate degree program would require that one faculty, or at most two or three faculties, take responsibility for much if not all course delivery. This is what happened at Osaka University.

We could not fail to admire the ingenuity of the Japanese government and the Ministry of Education, Culture, Sports, Science, and Technology, (MEXT) for coming up with the Global 30 Project as it was one sure way of ensuring that a lot more than lip service was paid to internationalizing teaching and learning in the top Japanese universities. Each new G30 program would require considerable internationalizing of procedures, and teaching and learning.

At Osaka University we committed ourselves to creating two undergraduate programs. One was the Chemistry and Biology Combined Major Program (CBCMP) and this was designed and then delivered by three science schools: the Graduate School of Science, the Graduate School of Engineering, and the Graduate School of Engineering Science. The other program was our one, the

---

2) Higher Education Quality Assurance Principles for the Asia-Pacific region, a set of draft principles drawn up as the Workshop on Higher Education Quality Assurance in the Asia-Pacific held in Chiba City, Japan on 18, February 2008. Available at http://internationaleducation.gov.au/About-AEI/Policy/Documents/Brisbane%20Communique/Quality_Assurance_Principles_pdf.pdf Last accessed 3 January, 2015.

Figure 1.1 *First recruitment brochure for the Human Sciences International Undergraduate Degree program.*

Human Sciences All-English Undergraduate Degree Program. This was subsequently re-named the Human Sciences International Undergraduate Degree Program. It is usually abbreviated as the HUS program in keeping with how students themselves started to refer to the program.

The HUS program is composed of two majors, Contemporary Japan and Global Citizenship, which students decide upon in their third year. Both majors are social science based and require students to take introductory disciplinary courses in Sociology, Anthropology, Economics, and Politics. At the same time,

Figure 1.2 *2014 recruitment brochure for the Human Sciences International Undergraduate Degree program*

in the first two years of the program students take a wide range of skill-based courses including Critical Thinking, Academic Writing, Presentation Skills, Data Processing Skills, Statistics for Social Science Research, Qualitative Research Methods, and Quantitative Research Methods. Other required courses include Contemporary Japan, Global Citizenship, International Education and Gender Studies. Overall, the program is highly demanding in terms of English language skills, particularly due to the interactive teaching and learning environment that we all strive to provide.

The program has been highly evaluated by students and we have enjoyed growing numbers of applications from prospective students over the past four years. From feedback it would seem that the clarity of learning outcomes and high quality of the courses have contributed to the success of the program to date. The quality assurance framework that has sustained the program and the hands-on experience of delivering a high quality program are the subject matter of this Handbook.

Visualizing 'Quality' Practice

While in the early days of the program we freely banded around the terms 'quality' and 'quality' assurance, we had not theorized in any way what they meant. Now, over four year later, we realise that we instinctively employed two quality concepts in the scaffolding that we developed for the program. The first was '**quality as threshold**'. Here 'quality defines minimum standards' usually involving 'broad definitions of desired knowledge, skills and attitudes of graduates' (McKimm, 2009, p. 187). Tools that we used for this, as you will see in the next chapter, include setting **graduate attributes** (skills and attributes we expected to nurture in all our students by the time they graduated); working with **benchmark statements** for both majors (clear indications of minimum standards that have to be reached to gain a degree in a particular disciplinary area); and threshold level learning outcomes. We hoped and expected our students to go beyond these, but we wanted to create a clear, transparent and measurable minimum level that our students would reach before being awarded a degree in Human Sciences.

The second quality concept that we instinctively employed was that of '**quality as enhancement**'. This 'emphasizes continuous improvement' and 'centres on the idea that achieving quality is essential' to any HE program and stresses the responsibility of program providers to do this while making best use of autonomy and academic freedom of teachers' delivering the program (see McKimm, 2009, p. 187). As you will see in Part One, the activities we have and continue to engage in include regular **core group meetings** made of the key team of instructors and academic affairs administrative personnel to discuss the program, the students, shared issues and concerns; **PD sessions** for instructors new to EMI or the idea of learning as an interactive process; **moderation meetings** to ensure reliability of assessment; and semester end reflections on practice through the writing of **course leader reports**.

Judy McKimm identifies in total six sub-categories of the quality concept in HE and to a greater or lesser extent these are also functioning and informing our practice on the Human Sciences International Undergraduate Degree Program. These are quality as practice, quality as 'zero errors', quality as 'fitness for purpose', and 'quality as transformation' (2009, p. 187). Quality as excellence, which seeks to demonstrate higher standards by surpassing threshold standards is a traditional view on quality. We certainly aim to scaffold **'quality as excellence'** by recognizing outcomes that clearly demonstrate that a student has well exceeded threshold level. We are able to demonstrate this with criteria based grading that links assessments tightly in with learning outcomes at any particular level of the program. From the beginning we aimed to set thresholds, but also to reach for excellence. This dual vison, we believe, has strengthened our approach and the program.

Setting the Context of English-Medium Programs

Japan is one of a number of countries in Asia that first started to introduce English language courses and then, more recently whole degree programs in English in order to attract a wider segment of the globally mobile international student body (Byun and Kim, 2011; Lassegard, 2006; Tsuneyoshi, 2005). As a result of the G30 program and related government policy, the number of EMI delivered degree programs has greatly increased. In particular there has been an increase in EMI undergraduate programs. Before the G30 project, in 2008, there were five universities in Japan offering undergraduate degree programs with English as the medium of instruction (one public and four private). In the same year there were 68 universities offering 128 graduate degree programs (MEXT, 2008). Since then an additional, 33 undergraduate and 123 graduate-level EMI degree programs are now being offered in Japan (MEXT, 2014).

As mentioned earlier, delivering a full undergraduate degree program is far more challenging to universities than a graduate program, so the increase in EMI undergraduate courses in Japan poses some significant challenges for Japanese HEIs. There may be language issues on the side of both the instructors and the students. A significant proportion of students may be working in a second or even third language and have varying degrees of proficiency. On the one hand, universities may have difficulty finding instructors who are able to comfortable deliver a whole course in English. There may be a heavy reliance on bringing in specially hired staff in large numbers to deliver such programs, which creates challenges at all sorts of levels, not least bringing them together as a team. At the same time, these EMI programs are conducted in the context of a dominant Japanese language environment and this makes it more difficult for students to quickly reach the desired English proficiency level. There are also concerns that students on English language programs are isolated from their peers and are not able to access the full benefits of university life (Bradford, 2012; Burgess et al., 2010). Students may not be overly familiar with the styles of teaching and learning that are more common in EMI programs (Bradford, 2012; Tsuneyoshi, 2005).

While this Handbook cannot address all these issues, it hopes to offer ideas that will help program providers and course instructors to deliver a course that not only meets minimum threshold standards but goes well beyond this. It hopes to achieve this by providing practical ideas about how to scaffold quality teaching and learning in the context of EMI programs. While the ideas here may not resolve all the challenges of EMI, we feel they are an important step in the right direction.

The Purpose of this Handbook

Our primary aim in updating and expanding the original *The Osaka University Teaching Quality Handbook: A Guide to Best Practices in the Provision of Teaching and Assessment for Undergraduate Degree Programs* is to make available to a wider audience the theory and practice that we have employed in developing and implementing one EMI undergraduate program that has met with a degree of success. Much of the literature about the delivery of EMI programs and courses in the Japanese context offers a largely negative picture that focuses overwhelmingly on identifying possible problems and fails to suggest or explore possible solutions that may be employed to ameliorate these (e.g., Bradford, 2012; Burgess et al., 2010; Mori, 2011). These studies are not based on practice or, in many cases, a particularly thorough research methodology. This Handbook, of course, is not a research output, but a practical guide to how to deliver high equality EMIs in the Japanese or wider Asian context. It is informed by theory and practice that has come from HE in the UK and reworks the latter for the different institutional and cultural setting.

This Handbook has been written to inform practice. It presents materials that may guide and inform program providers and instructors on key features of effective teaching, learning and assessment associated with high quality delivery of undergraduate level courses. The particular focus of the Handbook is to provide tools and techniques that we hope will assist in the development and delivery of undergraduate education in countries that may not have strong traditions in internal, program level quality assurance practices, even if broader QA structures are in place. In particular, the authors draw on their experience in designing, implementing and assessing an English-medium based undergraduate degree program in Human Sciences offered by the School of Human Sciences, Osaka University, Japan. The pedagogical approach adopted here stresses the interlinked nature of course delivery, assessment, feedback and development, and is explicitly directed towards establishing a clear and measurable link between the design and implementation of individual courses and program level outcomes.

For example, should program administrators require that graduates of a given undergraduate degree program be able to exhibit a range of skills, abilities, knowledge and personal characteristics upon successful completion (i.e., program level criteria), it is then crucial that individual courses are designed and implemented that provide for such criteria to be achieved. With the growing internationalization of higher education and diversification of the student body it is important to establish clear frameworks for the provision and evaluation of high quality university teaching and assessment, both within and between institutions, to ensure that:

- Assessments concerning a given degree qualification can be made accurately.
- Awarding of grades (at both course and program level) adequately measure and reflect the skills and abilities of students.
- Comparisons can be made between comparable qualifications at different institutions.
- Clear frameworks enable instructors to design and implement courses that ensure students can demonstrate achievement of desired knowledge and skills.

We strongly believe that the practices outlined here, while developed in the context of the Human Sciences, will offer insights to program providers and instructors across the disciplines. While the Handbook particularly focuses on undergraduate teaching, we have applied ideas here that were originally used successfully by us in graduate level teaching. So we would suggest that these are flexible and potentially provide good scaffolding for teaching and learning excellence at lower or higher degree level.

Navigating the Handbook

The broad topics covered in this Handbook are as follows:

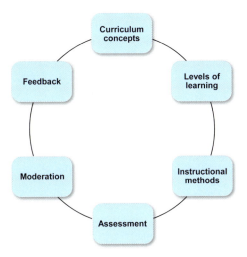

Figure 1.3 *Handbook topics.*

The main focus of the book is to provide guidance on the design and delivery of undergraduate education that stresses the interlinked nature of instructional methods, course assessment, moderation practices and approaches to learning. In short, an integrated and aligned approach is stressed. Further, the approach presented here does not assume that such integration and alignment can be delivered in a complete form prior to program delivery, as we believe this to be an on-going process.

Questions that we consider to be vital include:
- What is the purpose of my course?
- What do I expect students to learn (knowledge and skills) from taking my course?
- What teaching methods are effective for the delivery of the specific course content?
- What methods of assessment will best facilitate learning and provide clear evidence of learning?
- How can evaluating student work (individual assessment items and overall

course grades) be undertaken?
- How does my course fit within a program (e.g., degree)?
- How can my course be tailored to suit a range of diverse expectations and needs of students (e.g., international students, students from culturally diverse backgrounds)?
- How can I effectively utilize teaching assistants to better deliver my course?
- How can I improve my courses over time?

We hope that some of the concepts and suggestions may inform and assist you in the process of designing, implementing, assessing and evaluating your courses.

Getting Started

While materials presented here have been developed and utilized for a specific degree program in Japan (the Human Sciences International Undergraduate Degree offered by Osaka University) they may be useful in developing best practices for other undergraduate degree programs offered in Japan and the Asia-Pacific region.

A Final Word

The authors of this book have considerable experience teaching and learning in the British, Australian and Japanese higher education systems and have sorted through the wealth of data on evidence-based approaches to improving higher education quality. We have sought to incorporate (wherever possible) best practice in the provision of undergraduate social science courses, drawn from recent work in the United States, the United Kingdom, Australia and Japan. Clearly there are large cultural differences in the delivery of higher education across these countries, but some commonly agreed standards and practices can be identified. This book brings together these best practices in a compact single volume. The information and advice contained within these pages are not meant to be 'written in stone', but are offered to provide a platform from which different program providers and course instructors can begin to think about the design, implementation and evaluation of their own programs. We hope that in synthesizing information concerning best practices for practical use in this book you may find some helpful suggestions for your own teaching and learning practices.

References

Bradford, A. (2013). English-medium degree programs in Japanese universities: learning from the European experience. *Asian Education and Development Studies, 2*(3), 225-240.

Byun, K. and Kim, M. (2011). Shifting patterns of the government's policies for the internationalization of Korean higher education. *Journal of Studies in International Education, 15*(5), 467-486.

Burgess, C., Gibson, I., Klaphake, J. and Selzer, M. (2010). The 'Global 30' Project and Japanese higher education reform: An example of a 'closing in' or an 'opening up'? *Globalisation, Societies and Education, 8*(4), 461–475.

Gürüz, K. (2011). *Higher education and international student mobility in the global knowledge economy. (2nd Ed.).* Albany, NY: State University of New York Press.

Knight, J. (2008) *Higher education in turmoil: The changing world of internationalization.* Rotterdam, The Netherlands: Sense Publishers. (p. 21).

Kuwamura, A. (2009). The challenges of increasing capacity and diversity in Japanese higher education through proactive recruitment strategies. *Journal of Studies in International Education, 13* (2), 189-202.

Lassegard, J. P. (2006). International student quality and Japanese higher education reform. *Journal of Studies in International Education, 10*(2), 119-140.

McKimm, J. (2009). Quality, standards and enhancement. In H. Fry, S. Ketteridge and S. Marshall (Eds.), *A handbook for teaching and learning in higher education: Enhancing academic practice. (3rd Ed.).* New York: Routledge.

MEXT. (2008). *White Paper on Education, Culture, Sports, Science and Technology.* [http://www.mext.go.jp/b_menu/hakusho/html/hpab200801/1292564.htm]

MEXT. (2014). *Global 30: Present and future.* Paper presented at the Global 30 Symposium.

Mori, J. (2011). G30 and its implications for Japan. *University of Kyoto International Exchange Center Journal, 1*, 63-71.

Tsuneyoshi, R. (2005). Internationalization strategies in Japan. *Journal of Research in International Education, 4* (1), 65-86.

Yamamoto, B. and Bysouth, D. (2011). *Osaka University Teaching Quality Handbook: A Guide to Best Practice in the Provision of Teaching and Assessment for Undergraduate Degree Programmes.* Osaka University: Osaka.

Yamamoto, B. and Bysouth, D. (2013). *Osaka University Teaching Quality Handbook: A Guide to Best Practice in the Provision of Teaching and Assessment for Undergraduate Degree Programmes (Second Edition).* Osaka University: Osaka.

Yamamoto, B.A., Ishikura Y. and Bysouth D. (2012). *A Pebble that creates great waves: Global 30 classes and internationalisation of the student body.* Conference paper presented at the 8th QS Asia Pacific Professional Leaders in Education Conference, The Westin Resort Nusa Dua, Bali, Indonesia, 14-16 November, 2012.

Part One

Creating the Framework for Enhancing the Quality of English-Medium Programs and Courses

Beverley A. Yamamoto
Don Bysouth

Two

Scaffolding Quality
– Key Curriculum Concepts

Benchmarking

The **terminology** of benchmark standards and statements, although now used by educational institutions all over the world, is specifically associated with quality assurance activities in the United Kingdom (UK). A benchmark refers to a **point of reference or standard**, and benchmarking is a key tool in the evaluation of program standards.

Benchmarking has been used extensively by institutions of higher education in the UK in order to define the knowledge, skills and abilities that can be expected of a student graduating from any given undergraduate or graduate degree program in a particular subject area. The Quality Assurance Agency for Higher Education (QAA[1]) in the UK has been central to this process by commissioning Benchmarking Groups to undertake the task of drawing up benchmarks by discipline/subject at different degree levels. According to the QAA, the aim of benchmarking is to 'provide a means for the academic community to describe the nature and characteristics of programs in a specific subject or subject area. They also represent general expectations about standards for the award of qualifications at a given level in terms of attributes and capabilities that those possessing should have demonstrated'[2]. As these can change through time, benchmarking is always subject to a regular review process.

---

1) www.qaa.ac.uk
2) *Area Studies, 2008 Benchmark Statements*, The Quality Assurance Agency for Higher Education. (http://www.qaa.ac.uk/Publications/InformationAndGuidance/Documents/areastudies08.pdf)

Benchmarking activities embody a 'quality as threshold' concept of quality assurance where minimum standards are set for the acquisition of a degree in any given subject that can be employed across institutions. It involves 'broad definitions of desired knowledge, skills and attitudes of graduates' (McKimm, 2009).

To a certain extent subject benchmark statements have also been created to provide prospective students and graduate employers with information about the nature and standards of awards in a given subject or subject area. This is not their **ultimate purpose**, however, as benchmark standards are an essential tool for program designers and those working on higher education quality assurance. The idea is not to lay down a curriculum for all to follow, but to provide standards and indicators by subject area at different degree levels that different universities can flexibly and innovatively use to create, implement and evaluate programs. The goal is to assure high quality programs are delivered by all program providers.

For example, in the design of our Human Sciences International Undergraduate Degree Program at Osaka University we have drawn on the benchmark statements compiled for undergraduate honours degree programs in Area Studies (for the Contemporary Japan major) and International Relations (for the Global Citizenship major). By using these benchmark statements as a guide, not only have we been able to draw on the expertise of UK Benchmarking Groups we have also created a framework, perhaps for the first time in Japan, that would enable the **external evaluation** or **moderation** of a program. It is feasible we could seek an external evaluation by a UK institution of higher education in the very near future with these benchmarks. Alternatively, we could seek evaluation by another institution in Japan were it familiar with the benchmarking criteria. The following benchmarks are presented for the Contemporary Japan major.

Benchmark statements for the Contemporary Japan Major, Human Sciences International Undergraduate Degree Program, Osaka University

---

In setting the benchmarks and learning outcomes for the Contemporary Japan Major a clear distinction will be made between **knowledge** and **understanding** on the one hand and **skill acquisition** (generic or transferable skills and subject-specific skills) on the other.

The Bachelor degree in Human Sciences, Contemporary Japan Major will promote knowledge and understanding of:

- Japan through an interdisciplinary approach, including its history, culture, designated geographic area past and present, and current social issues
- Japan within regional and world contexts
- relevant scholarship originating from both within and outside Japan
- the dynamics of social change within Japan and the East Asia region
- the different disciplinary perspectives that can be taken to studying one or more aspects of Japan
- key methods and concepts for understanding different subject matter

The Bachelor degree in Human Sciences, Contemporary Japan Major will promote the following subject specific and generic skills:

Subject Specific Skills

- an ability to critically engage with the study of Japan from a number of disciplinary and interdisciplinary approaches
- the ability to compare and contrast the appropriateness of different disciplinary approaches
- the ability to form a research question/problem and apply a suitable methodology to elicit data relevant to addressing and finding solutions to this question
- the ability to use and critically interrogate a range of primary and secondary written and/or oral and/or visual sources, in their original language where appropriate
- skills in the construction of bibliographies, library and internet research skills, proficiency in reading and analysis of texts both in English and to a lesser extent in Japanese, and the abilities in the analysis of visual and aural material as a medium for understanding another culture
- first language (L1) or near-L1 level skills in the English language and functioning skills in the Japanese language to enable research of primary sources.

Generic Skills

- read and use materials both incisively and with sensitivity to compare and contrast ideas and concepts found within different disciplinary and geographical contexts
- identify and resolve problems
- communicate ideas with clarity, coherence, and persuasiveness
- synthesize information, adopt critical appraisals and develop reasoned argument based on such appraisals

- select and apply appropriate methodologies and theories
- critically reflect upon the scope and limitations of what has been ascertained and understood
- analyze issues proficiently in the light of evidence and argument
- work with a significant amount of independence, demonstrated self-direction, self-management and intellectual initiative both in learning and studying and in time management
- present materials orally in a clear and effective manner, using audio-visual aids, where appropriate, and answering questions from an audience
- listen effectively and work creatively, flexibly, and adaptively with others

Note that such benchmark statements are used to establish learning outcomes for individual programs and within programs at each level. We will now move on to consider learning outcomes.

Learning Outcomes

Learning outcomes refer to the **specific intentions of a given course of study** at different levels or stages in that program or different courses or modules upon completion. What are your expectations for what students will learn in a single course? What are your expectations across several courses in a semester or term? What are the expectations on the completion of a year, or an entire degree program? Like benchmark statements, learning outcomes are student and learning focused, and relate to both skill- and knowledge-based expectations. Program learning outcomes should be aligned with benchmark statements and provide measurable standards for program providers and evaluators to work with. Individual course- or module-based learning outcomes should in turn align with the learning outcomes for the program at each level (we provide an example in the following section).

Establishing clear learning outcomes for individual programs at each stage (in the Japanese context this is likely to be by year group) can assist students in their learning (i.e., they have a clear understanding of what is expected of them at particular stages of the program), helps educators develop and implement teaching strategies that will provide opportunities for the students to achieve the desired program outcomes, and provides a guide for students and employers about the skills, knowledge and understanding achieved upon successful course completion.

Each module or course in a program must **align its learning outcomes** with that of the program at that stage. This is a very different way of thinking about course delivery as it becomes essential to plan how each course and all courses together achieve the learning outcomes for the program. Thus it demands consideration of a number of different ways of working than have hitherto been followed in many Japanese universities. While the Japanese system offers enormous flexibility and allows educators to do what they know best or feel most confident teaching, the system may resemble a potluck party. If all goes well you get a good balance of dishes that blend well together. However, if luck is not on your side you can end up with many similar offerings that fail to satisfy the appetite and may even upset the system.

The learning outcomes concept should not rigidly impose a teaching style or even teaching content on an educator, but refocuses him or her away from themselves (away from the question what am I going to teach) and toward the student (what does he or she need to have learned in terms of skills and knowledge by the end of the course and what role does my course/module play in building towards these ultimate learning outcomes?).

When **developing and implementing learning outcomes** the following should be considered:

> Learning outcomes are clearly identified and communicated to students

> Learning opportunities are clearly designed to enable students to achieve the specified learning outcomes

> Assessment is designed to allow students to demonstrate achievement of the specified learning outcomes

As previously stressed, individual courses should have their learning outcomes aligned with the learning outcomes for the program at each level. Here we show the learning outcomes for the first year (Level One) of the Human Sciences International Undergraduate Program, Contemporary Japan Major. For the less familiar skills-based outcomes we have provided concrete examples of how to make them measurable. Note how these are leading directly to the benchmarks for this major. Also note the use of the use of various performance and achievement verbs in the articulation of the learning outcome.

> **Examples of learning outcomes for the Contemporary Japan Major, Human Sciences International Undergraduate Program**

Level One

Students acquire sound descriptive knowledge of basic concepts and begin to evaluate information in a critical manner as demonstrated in small group discussion, essays and quizzes.

Skills

SK1 Demonstrate the ability to interpret, evaluate and present scholarly arguments on a specific topic in an appropriate academic manner.

> Eg. Students produce a scholarly essay on an assigned topic with reference to key sources covered in class, and at the upper level of attainment utilize some additional secondary sources.

SK2 With a degree of confidence, begin to critically engage with source material in order to accurately summarize key themes/topics in a presentation format.

> Eg. Students can prepare and deliver a brief presentation on an assigned topic to a small group and answer questions with a degree of confidence. At the upper level of attainment students utilize a range of media and technology and draw upon a range of secondary sources.

SK3 Demonstrate an improvement in Japanese language ability relative to the student's starting point.

> Eg. Students starting at entry level should complete the 100 and 200 level program over the course of the year. Those students starting at higher levels should make a similar level of progress in relative terms.

SK4 With some direction, complete course work using appropriate computer software, including word processing and Power Point applications.

> Eg. Students produce a polished piece of writing or a presentation that makes use of basic level data processing skills. At the upper level, the student should be able to make use of some of the more advanced functions of word processing, and Power Point programs.

SK5 Demonstrate the ability to make a positive contribution in formal and informal small group environments in various roles.

> Eg. In problem-solving exercises the student should show an ability to work together productively and fairly as a group.

SK6 Demonstrate the ability to work independently and in a self-directed manner through appropriate planning, time management, and completion of course work while adjusting to life in Japan as full-time undergraduate students.

Knowledge and understanding
K1 Demonstrate a basic understanding of different interpretations of Japanese culture and society.
K2 Distinguish between disciplinary perspectives on key social issues pertaining to Japanese society.
K3 Identify the key characteristics of different periods in Japanese history.
K4 Recognize different insider and outsider views of contemporary Japanese society and locate them historically.
K5 Recognize the key characteristics of different disciplinary approaches used to understand Japanese culture and society.
K6 Identify key globalizing processes impacting on Japanese society at various levels in the 21st century and discuss in an informed manner areas of increasing Japanese influence in the world.
K7 Growing awareness of human rights and individual dignity in a global context.

Curriculum Alignment

One powerful way in which the various elements of any teaching program can be conceptualized and organized is by adopting the concept of curriculum alignment (Biggs and Tang, 2007). With curriculum alignment, rather than having courses, assessment, teaching practices and strategies operating in a more or less independent or *ad hoc* fashion, the various components and elements are integrated, or aligned, to form a coherent framework.

As Biggs and Tang (2007) have cogently argued, important components or elements that can benefit from alignment include:

- The taught curriculum.
- The teaching methods employed.
- The assessment procedures and reporting methods utilized.
- The interactional climate produced between instructors and students.
- The institutional climate.

For brevity, here we will restrict our suggestions to the **first three components** (see Figure 2.1). When alignment exists between desired learning outcomes, the methods used to teach and equip students with relevant knowledge and skills related to the outcomes, and the practices of assessing if students have met the desired outcomes, teaching will be more effective than if these elements are treated independently.

One simple way to understand this is to consider that educators should begin from establishing what the intended learning outcomes are for a given course, and then develop learning and teaching activities, with aligned assessment methods, that will best assist students achieving the desired learning outcomes. Note that this approach can be utilized to achieve alignment, not just within and between individual courses, but also alignment at the program level.

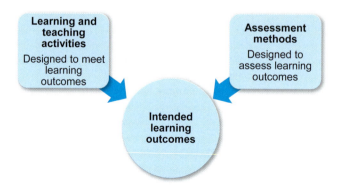

Figure 2.1 *Components of curriculum alignment (Biggs and Tang, 2007)*

Syllabus Writing

One of the most important documents for any course is the **course syllabus**. However, many practitioners only consider the importance of the syllabus in terms of its function as an administrative tool (i.e., it is a requirement that every course has a syllabus, regardless of what the syllabus contains). However, we would argue that a course syllabus is extremely important for a number of interrelated reasons. The course syllabus serves as a kind of "learning contract" and permanent record between professors and students (e.g., Parkes and Harris, 2002). It specifies what will be taught, how it will be taught, the assessment policies and general rules pertaining to the course. It also serves as a vital document for use in course and program development and evaluation. While these aspects are important, here we focus on how a syllabus can be utilized as a **learning tool**, for both students *and* professors.

Consider the following questions with regard to a course you may be planning to provide (Fry, Ketteridge and Marshall, 2009):

- What are your beliefs about the content and how it should be taught?
- What do the students need to be effective learners of your course content?
- What is the rationale for the course? How is it relevant for the students?
- What do you expect students to do in order to pass the course successfully?
- What skills, abilities or prior knowledge should the students possess?

The course syllabus need not serve simply as a guide to students taking your class (i.e., as a set of rules and obligations they must follow) but also as a guide that can assist you develop and implement what you consider to be important for the teaching of your particular subject matter.

Given there will be considerable variation in syllabi, depending on the type of course and content that may need to be covered, we suggest that a syllabus should (at a minimum) contain the following (we provide a sample syllabus and a syllabus template following this section):

- **Overview and aims of course**

This should provide sufficient information on the course that a potential student can make an informed decision about enrolling in the course. It is also useful to have a clear overview and aims so that, at the program level, determinations can be made concerning recommended enrolment patterns.

- **Course content**

This should give a general overview of what the course will cover. One useful thing to consider is that research indicates that providing too many topics is likely to impact negatively on students' attempts to learn the material in addition to creating considerable workload issues for instructors (e.g., Bransford et al., 2000). It can be helpful to reduce the amount of topics and materials you plan to present from an initial draft to the final version of the syllabus.

You can begin by thinking about the 'wider picture', 'grand narrative' or 'big idea' that may be central to your course, and then generating possible theme and topic areas that are logically linked to this. These can then provide a framework for the individual lessons or sessions that will help clarify what needs to be prepared and covered, in addition to providing a clear logical structure that students can follow.

- **Teaching methods**

While there is no need to provide an extensive rational for the kinds of teaching methods that will be utilized on the course, it can be helpful to give a brief list (e.g., particularly if you plan on using a range of methods). These can be articulated with some specificity when possible, particularly if unusual or novel teaching methods will be utilized.

- **Indicative reading**

This should specify any reading materials (i.e., textbooks) that students are required to obtain. In addition, it can be very helpful to list materials that the course will draw upon and provide information on a range of sources that might be useful for students to consult (i.e., journal titles, software, internet resources). Importantly, you should avoid merely listing required reading materials and try to provide some kind of structure that indicates to students how the readings are to be used. For example, do you want students to read a specific text prior to attending a weekly class session? Is a text presented as a general resource? Are elements of your course content linked specifically to particular texts? Providing this information will assist students to understand *why* you are asking them to read the material, and *how* the material might be understood in the context of the entire course.

- **Assessment methods**

These should be clearly defined and described. For example, if the course will involve formative assessment, how will such assessment be undertaken? For summative assessment detail should be provided on the form, length, scope, and grading policy employed. Providing limited information on the forms of assessment undertaken may negatively impact on student engagement and evaluation of the course overall, so it is important to provide clear information early in the course (e.g., Garvalia, Hummel, Wiley and Huitt, 1999). This will also reduce the amount of time required to later deal with student inquiries concerning the specific requirements of assessments.

- **Learning outcomes**

These can specify what knowledge and understanding a student should be able to demonstrate upon successful course completion, and may also include specific examples of skills, qualities, or attributes that a student may possess. Rather than treating learning outcomes as something that can be added to a course following the development of course content, it can be useful to develop possible learning outcomes at the initial design stage. What do you want students to learn from doing your course? Are these measurable? Will students be able to get a clear idea of what successful completion of the course might represent in terms of skills and knowledge?

Syllabus Tips

The following is a list of tips and suggestions, based on feedback from students and professors, on how to make your syllabi more effective. These tips are based on extensive feedback from students enrolled in *Human Sciences International Undergraduate Degree Program* courses. We have learned that if the syllabus is appropriate for the course you provide, students are likely to be more engaged and ultimately satisfied with the course. Students often complain when a syllabus does not accurately reflect either course content, course learning outcomes, course structure and/or assessment. Here, we just focus on the main sections that seem to be the most important based on quantitative and qualitative evaluations provided by students.

Course Overview

While this section does not need to be extensive, it is important to provide sufficient information about your course that a student can make an informed decision about enrolling in the course. It is also important to provide sufficient information about your course so that course designers can establish whether there are multiple courses with significant overlap, what the intended level of the course is (e.g., first year undergraduate or graduate level), and if there may be courses which should be taken prior to (or concurrently) with the course.

Tip
The strongest tip we could offer here would be to ensure that your course overview is understandable to students unfamiliar with the subject matter. In addition, if you deviate significantly from the course overview when teaching your course, students are likely to give poor evaluations and be concerned that the course they thought they were enrolling in was not the course that was actually delivered!

Course Learning Outcomes

Perhaps the most difficult part of the syllabus is constructing clear learning outcomes. These should list the knowledge and skills that students are expected to acquire from successful completion of your course. These should be measurable, and they should clearly be linked to both your course content and the course assessment. In other words, it helps establish that students 1) learn knowledge/skills that you want them to acquire, 2) the course content provides sufficient coverage of these, and 3) the assessment provides a reliable and valid measure of these knowledge/skills.

Tips
Too many outcomes and you have a risk that there will be too many things for students to cover, and you may not be able to adequately assess them.

Too few outcomes and you have a risk that much of your teaching will be considered unimportant, and you may find your assessment items simply assess the same one or two things.

For *knowledge and understanding* it can help to think about what kinds of traditional disciplinary knowledge the students should acquire (e.g., for a course on introductory sociology perhaps understandings or awareness of some basic theories would be an appropriate outcome).

For *skills, qualities and attributes* it can help to think of what you want students to be able to demonstrate by way of actions (e.g., for a course on introductory sociology it might include how to apply a basic theory in a particular way).

Course Content

Students seem to appreciate having the course content described in terms of weekly sessions, with a brief topic heading and some description about the topic. It can also be useful to include course readings here, or if you plan to provide readings during the session some indication of what will be provided. It can help students focus their reading if you add one or two questions to consider while reading.

Tip

An excellent (and relatively straightforward) way to communicate your course content is to use the following format:

> ***Week 1 Introduction to Sociology***
> In this session we will begin to explore some basic understandings of sociology, and consider some sociological topics.
> ***Readings:*** Chapter 1 of the textbook

This may allow you to provide a more structured overview of your course, and can help you identify logical 'sections' that might help students understand your organization of course content.

Teaching and Learning Methods

A brief indication of your style of teaching can really help students. For example, if you plan to provide a traditional lecture based course, you could simply indicate that sessions would be conducted as lectures. If you were mixing your teaching methods (e.g., giving lectures, seminars, practical sessions, group work) it can help to list these so that students are aware of what the course requirements are.

Tip

Here you can establish 'ground rules' for your course, so that students are aware of what your expectations are (e.g., if you stress group discussions then students have the responsibility to come prepared to interact).

It can be useful to include details on the 'total contact hours' for your course. For example, if you plan on delivering 15 x 90 minute sessions = 22.5 hours for a 15 week course.

Remember to include some indication of what your expectations are with regard to 'non-contact hours'. For example, if you plan on students doing 90 minutes per week for your course outside of class settings (e.g., reading, activities, working on assessments) you would allocate 22.5 hours here.

For example, in our Human Sciences International Undergraduate Degree Program we assume that a 2 credit point course will comprise 30 hours of study in a classroom setting (each session considered equal to 2 hours). This can give you an idea of what the likely workload for your course will be if students are enrolled in an average course load (12 courses per semester = 36-40 hours minimum).

Assessment

A list of the assessment and weighting should be provided here. In our experience students have given very favourable feedback when syllabi also provide some brief descriptions of each individual assessment task. Even if you have not decided the actual assessment items you will use, providing a brief example is extremely helpful for students – even if you intend on providing a more detailed description later in the course.

Tip

An effective way to provide a quick overview of the assessment is as follows:

> **Assessment**
> -Critical essay (2,000 words) 50%
> -Group presentation 40%
> -Class participation 10%
>
> The critical essay (2,000 words, 50%) will require you to provide an analysis of sociological data that will be provided on the topic of 'higher education in Japan'. (more details here…)
>
> The group presentation (40%) will require you to prepare and present a group presentation (using multimedia) of 15 minutes duration that explores the topic of (more details here…)
>
> Class participation (10%) will be assessed by (more details here…)

It is important that if you utilize class participation you provide specific information on how this will be assessed. Additionally, you should be clear on whether you are assessing 'attendance' (i.e., awarding marks for students turning up to classes) or 'participation' (i.e., students are explicitly graded according to some criteria). While this is true for all assessment strategies, one of the most common issues that students raise is that they do not understand how professors grade participation, so ensuring this is transparent and fair will likely lead to greater student engagement with both the course content and the assessment itself.

Writing a Course Syllabus

As we have considered, one obvious purpose of a syllabus is to communicate to your students what the course is about, why it is taught, how it is taught and where/when it is and of course what will be required of the students for them to complete the course with a passing grade. Beyond this, a good syllabus keeps you and your students on track and can alleviate problems of unclear goals and directions, and also provides an indication to students that you undertake teaching with a high degree of professionalism (Davis, 2009). Moreover, the quality of the syllabus can be (and is often) taken as an indicator of teaching quality and learning by both students and other professors. Therefore it is important to be as clear as possible about how you want your course to be presented in syllabus form. While there may be considerable variation in the content of syllabi given the need to satisfy specific disciplinary or administrative requirements, it is important that some consideration is given to how the syllabi could be profitably utilized by academic colleagues to develop their own course syllabi (e.g., ideas for course content, assessment strategies, and other relevant elements).

We have provided a sample course syllabus here that illustrates many of the important features discussed so far. In addition, following the sample syllabus we have provided a syllabus template which outlines the key sections of a comprehensive syllabus document. Note that our examples are drawn from actual documents utilized in the delivery of our courses – they have not been created as exemplars of perfect practice! We present course documentation on one course (Critical Thinking Skills) throughout this book in order to provide a more detailed example of how elements of syllabus construction, learning outcomes, assessment, criteria documentation, and student evaluations and feedback can proceed in practice.

Sample Syllabus
Critical Thinking Skills (First Year Course)

Critical Thinking Skills – Syllabus
Osaka University, International College

1. BASIC COURSE INFORMATION

Course Title:	Critical Thinking Skills
Course Code:	13A404
Semester:	2011 – 1 (G30)
Class Hours:	Monday – Period 4 (1.5 hours per week)
Language of Instruction:	English
Number of Credits:	2

2. PROGRAMMES CONTAINING THIS COURSE

Programme Title	Core/Elective	Level
All-English Human Science Programme	Core	1
Chemistry and Biology Combined Major	Elective	1

3. PRE- AND CO-REQUISITES
These are courses that you must have studied previously in order to take this course, or courses that you must study simultaneously.

None

4. COURSE STAFF

Instructor(s):	Dr Don Bysouth
E-mail:	bysouth@hus.osaka-u.ac.jp
Office Location:	G30 Professors Office, 3rd Floor Human Sciences, Suita
Office Hours:	Friday 10:30am-12:00pm

5. COURSE OVERVIEW

This course provides students with a range of tools and strategies for developing critical thinking skills that can be utilized in both university and everyday settings. The course draws on a range of disciplines to examine truth and knowledge claims by examining logic and reasoning, rhetoric and argumentation, perspective taking, propaganda and the integration and synthesis of ideas. In addition, the course will utilize ideas from enquiry based learning (EBL) to enable students to blend and generate ideas and empirical evidence from many different domains to enable an integrated approach to evaluating, challenging and generating claims. The course will also consider the role of critical thinking in relation to moral and ethical issues. Students will undertake a blend of individual and group based activities examining truth claims in scholarly and mainstream media materials. The course is interdisciplinary in scope and will draw on a range of disciplines including education, psychology and philosophy, and will consider materials drawn from both academic and everyday settings.

6. COURSE LEARNING OUTCOMES

6.1 Knowledge and Understanding. After studying this course you should be able to:
- Describe a range of thinking and learning strategies that foster critical thinking;
- Appreciate the value of critical thinking skills in both academic and everyday settings;
- Distinguish between different forms of argument and persuasion;
- Reflect upon and challenge your own thinking practices.

6.2 Skills, Qualities and Attributes. After studying this course you should be able to:
- Identify, analyse and evaluate factual claims in a range of domains;
- Identify rhetorical devices and strategies utilized in making truth claims;
- Recognize common fallacies in everyday reasoning;
- Use a range of resources, including primary research papers and information technology;
- Use evidence to support or challenge an argument;
- Demonstrate a range of transferable skills including oral and written communication, effective planning and organisation, and independence.

7. COURSE CONTENT

Week 1	**Introduction**
	What is critical thinking?
Week 2	**Identifying arguments**
	We will focus on how to identify an argument or claim
Week 3	**Descriptions and explanations**
	We will focus on how descriptions are constructed in producing claims
Week 4	**Clarity and credibility**
	We will examine how to assess the clarity of an argument
Week 5	**Rhetorical techniques I**
	We will examine various rhetorical techniques and fallacies
Week 6	**Rhetorical techniques II**
	Further examination of rhetorical techniques and fallacies
Week 7	**Fallacies I**
	We will examine various logical fallacies
Week 8	**Fallacies II**
	Further examination of logical fallacies
Week 9	**Rival causes workshop**
	Identifying rival causes in explanatory accounts
Week 10	**Critical reading and note-making**
	We will examine various techniques to aid in critical reading
Week 11	**Critical writing**
	We will examine various techniques to aid critical writing
Week 12	**Case Study**
	Detailed interrupted case study
Week 13	**Moral and ethical reasoning**
	We will consider moral/ethical approaches to critical thinking
Week 14	**Ethical Case Study**
	We will analyse a case study involving an ethical dilemma
Week 15	**Revision/Review**
	Review of course topics and materials

8. TEACHING AND LEARNING METHODS

The course will be delivered utilizing a blend of mini-lectures, practical activities, workshops, group discussions and interrupted case studies. In addition the course delivery will feature elements of enquiry-based learning. Sessions will involve extensive use of audio-visual materials. Students will be provided with extensive handouts.

8.1 Range of modes of direct contact

Total contact hours:	22.5

8.2 Range of other learning methods

Total non-contact hours:	22.5

9. LEARNING RESOURCES

9.1 Textbooks

While there is no 'set' textbook required for this course, students are encouraged to obtain a recent textbook or workbook on 'critical thinking'. The following texts are recommended as useful references:

- Browne, N., & Keeley, S. (2011). *Asking the right questions: International edition. (10th Ed)*. Pearson.

- Cottrell, S. (2005). *Critical thinking skills*. Palgrave Macmillan.

- Moore, B.N., & Parker, R. (2011). *Critical thinking (10th Ed)*. McGraw-Hill.

9.2 Other Recommended Resources

Students will be provided with book chapters, readings and activity materials throughout the course from a range of materials, including the following:

- Connolly, P., Keller, D., Leever, M., & White, B. (2009). *Ethics in action: A case based approach*. Wiley-Blackwell.

In addition, materials drawn from peer reviewed journals, general literature, and film and audio materials will be utilized for critical engagement and discussion throughout the course.

10. ASSESSMENT

Assessment:
- Critical analysis of editorial (20%)
- Critical essay of 1,500 words (30%)
- Critical thinking portfolio (40%)
- Class participation (10%)

The course will be assessed by formative and summative assessment. Formative assessment will be undertaken throughout the term and consist of short practical exercises and group discussions. The summative assessment will comprise a critical thinking portfolio (40%), a critical essay (30%) and critical analysis of an editorial (20%). In addition, class participation will comprise 10% of the final course grade.

The critical thinking portfolio will be a written portfolio, submitted at the end of term, which will comprise completed set activities, reflective commentary and other self-directed work relating to critical thinking. The critical essay will require students to construct and defend an argument on a topic to be negotiated with instructor. The critical analysis of editorial will require students to select a recent editorial from a mainstream publication (either print or electronic) and provide a detailed critique (no more than 1,000 words) of the arguments presented in the editorial. In addition, class participation will comprise 10% of the final course grade.

Students will be provided with detailed information on assessment including information on how assessment rationale and marking are related to course learning outcomes.

All assessment items will be moderated.

10.1 Assessment requirements

➤ Attendance at 80% of all sessions is required.

➤ Academic misconduct (cheating, collusion, plagiarism or falsification of information) in all forms of written work, lab tests, demonstrations, designs, presentations, in-class tests and examination can lead to consequences ranging from loss of marks in the relevant course to zero grades for all classes taken that semester.

10.2 Grading policy

Students will be awarded grades for performance in accordance with the following scheme:

Grade	Mark	Description
S	90~100	Pass
A	80~89	
B	70~79	
C	60~69	
F	0~59	Fail

Part One | Creating the Framework for Enhancing the Quality of English-Medium Programs and Courses

Syllabus Template with Instructions

Syllabus Template

1. BASIC COURSE INFORMATION

Course Title:	
Course Code:	
Semester:	
Class Hours:	
Language of Instruction:	
Number of Credits:	

2. PROGRAMMES CONTAINING THIS COURSE

Programme Title	Core/Elective	Level

3. PRE- AND CO-REQUISITES

These are courses that must have studied previously in order to take this course, or courses that must be studied simultaneously.

4. COURSE STAFF

Instructor(s):	
E-mail:	
Office Location:	
Office Hours:	

5. COURSE OVERVIEW

This should provide sufficient information on the course that a potential student can make an informed decision about enrolling in the course. It is also useful to have a clear overview and aims so that, at the programme level, determinations can be made concerning recommended enrollment patterns.

6. COURSE LEARNING OUTCOMES

Learning outcomes describe what you should know and be able to do by the end of the course. These may also include specific examples of skills, qualities, or attributes that a student may possess.

6.1 Knowledge and Understanding. After studying this course you should be able to:

6.2 Skills, Qualities and Attributes. After studying this course you should be able to:

7. COURSE CONTENT

This should give a general overview of what the course will cover.

8. TEACHING AND LEARNING METHODS

While there is no need to provide an extensive rational for the kinds of teaching methods that will be utilized on the course, it can be helpful to give a brief list (e.g. particularly if you plan on using a range of methods). These can be articulated with some specificity when possible, particularly if novel teaching methods will be utilized.

8.1 Range of modes of direct contact
This indicates the range of direct contact teaching and learning methods used on this course (e.g., lectures, seminars).

Total contact hours:

8.2 Range of other learning methods
This indicates the range of other teaching and learning methods used on this course (e.g., directed reading, research).

Total non-contact hours:

9. LEARNING RESOURCES
This should specify any required materials (i.e. textbooks) that students are required to obtain. In addition, it can be very helpful to list materials that the course will draw upon andn provide information on a range of sources that might be useful for students to consult (i.e. journal titles, software, internet resource).

9.1 Textbooks

9.2 Other Recommended Resources

10. ASSESSMENT
These should be clearly defined and described. For example, if the course will involve formative assessment, how will such assessment be undertaken? For summative assessment detail should be provided on the form, length, scope, and grading policy employed.

10.1 Assessment requirements
Here you should detail the specific policy for your course. It can also be useful to include a section (similar to the example given below) that details your policy on academic misconduct (e.g., plagiarism).

➢ Academic misconduct (cheating, collusion, plagiarism or falsification of information) in all forms of written work, lab tests, demonstrations, designs, presentations, in-class tests and examination can lead to consequences ranging from loss of marks in the relevant course to zero grades for all classes taken that semester.

10.2 Grading policy

Here you should provide clear guidelines specifying how grades will be awarded. It can also be useful to include a guide to how final grades or marks will be reported (as with the example provided below).

Grade	Mark	Description
S	90~100	Pass
A	80~89	
B	70~79	
C	60~69	
F	0~59	Fail

Constructing Learning Outcomes

While you might think descriptions of the course content may be the most important component of a syllabus, we would stress that detailed **learning outcomes** are perhaps as, if not more, important. These are particularly important to consider in the early design phases of a course, as they will provide a framework for course content, instructional methods and course assessment policies.

Clear learning outcomes are very important because they help us decide **what** we should teach, **how** best to teach and how to best **assess learning**. Learning outcomes describe the measurable knowledge, skills, abilities, or values that students should be able to demonstrate once upon the completion of the course. Imagine if you can tell students what you expect them to do, and give them opportunities to practice, then there is a good chance that they will be able to achieve these goals on assignment tasks. As a result, it is more likely they will learn what you want them to know.

What Do Clear Learning Outcomes Look Like?

Consider the previously outlined goals of learning outcomes that they should be:

- **Specific**
- **Measurable**
- **Realistic**

While program designers may be focused on how these learning outcomes are specific, measurable and realistic over an entire degree program, for most practitioners the focus will be on single courses undertaken in a single semester. One approach that might assist when you begin drafting your specific learning outcomes is to consider the level at which your outcomes need to be set.

Levels of Learning Outcomes[3]

---

3) Detailed version can be obtained from the University of South Carolina (http://www.sc.edu/cte/learningoutcomes/)

	Degree Program	**Course**	**Class Module**
Scope	Broad	Moderate	Narrow
Time Needed	One or more years	Weeks or months	Hours or days
Use	Design Curriculum	Design units of instruction	Design lectures, class exercises

If you are designing a single course your scope needs to be *moderate*. That is, you cannot hope to cover content that might be covered across several related courses, but you need to provide sufficient content that covers a number of sequential class modules. Often courses are designed with a focus on the individual class modules (e.g., single lectures) and the broader aims are developed later, often after a course has been run for the first time. However, time spent on the early design of a course may well provide a more coherent course, and for more integration at the individual class module level.

How to Develop Clear Learning Outcomes for a Specific Syllabus?

It can be helpful to think of each learning outcome as comprising a **learning statement**. These statements can have a general kind of format, which can allow the construction of quite specific learning outcomes. While it can be difficult and time consuming to do this a first time and for a single course, you can often recycle previously generated learning statements and adapt them to other courses.

Format of the Learning Outcome Statement

All learning outcomes have a common format:

> **Subject (S)   +   Verb (V)   +   Object (O)**

The **Subject** refers to the specific learner or student.
Each **Verb** represents a cognitive, affective or psychomotor domain which involves knowledge retention or transfer. [e.g., 'identify', 'consider', 'design']
Object is derived from the course content. [Different types of knowledge]

> **Examples of learning outcome statements**
> - *Students* will be able to *apply the principles of Industrial Organization and Operations Management to the healthcare supply chain.*
> - *You* will be able to *restructure the relationships between various IO theories according to the specificity of the healthcare environment* and *identify* dominant ones.

When writing the learning outcomes, you might find it useful to carefully consider how learning can be categorized as belonging to different domains (for example cognitive, affective and psychomotor). While there are many different ways in which learning might be characterized (the taxonomy utilized here is clearly psychological in orientation) what is important is that utilizing a taxonomy of learning can assist when constructing and evaluating learning outcomes, teaching methods and assessment practices, by providing a means by which one can describe *what* is to be learnt and *how* it is to be learnt.

It can be helpful to describe the learning that will result from an *activity*, using *precise terms* and *everyday words* (Davis, 2009). Remember, students may not be able to understand what they are supposed to learn if the learning statements are vague, full of technical jargon and written in complex language.

Example:

Category (e.g.)	Action Verbs & Cognitive Processes	Assessment Formats
Remember retrieve relevant knowledge from long-term memory	**Recognizing** comparing knowledge from long-term memory with presented information **Verbs** for learning outcome can be: identity, recognize, select, label…	True-false; multiple choice; Matching items from two lists
Analyse break materials into its constituent parts and determine how the parts relate to one another and to an overall structure or propose	**Organizing** determining how elements fit within a structure. **Verbs** for learning outcome can be: analyse, organize, outline…	Providing an outline, table, matrix, or hierarchical diagram

When writing course learning outcomes, some useful questions to ask are:

- How do you **observe** or **measure**:
  Knowledge?
  Skills?
  Proficiency?
  Commitment?
  Awareness?
- What are the tasks through which they can be observed?
- What are the actions that demonstrate these attributes?

Another important consideration is: how many learning outcomes do you think students can realistically achieve by the end of your course (Lowman, 1995)? We will consider the importance of having some kind of learning taxonomy in more detail in the following section.

References

Biggs, J. and Tang, C. (2007). *Teaching for quality learning at university (3rd Ed.)*. Maidenhead: Open University Press/McGraw Hill.

Bransford, J.D. et al. (2000). *How people learn: Brain, mind, experience and school.* Washington DC: National Academy Press.

Davis, B.G. (2009). *Tools for teaching (2nd Ed.).* San Francisco: Jossey-Bass.

Fry, H., Ketteridge, S. and Marshall, S. (Eds.). (2009). *A handbook for teaching and learning in higher education: Enhancing academic practice. (3rd Ed.)*. New York: Routledge.

Garvalia, L., Hummel, J., Wiley, L. and Huitt, W. (1999). Constructing the course syllabus: Faculty and student perceptions of important syllabus components. *Journal of Excellence in College Teaching, 10*(1), 5-22.

Lowman, J. (1995). *Mastering the techniques of teaching. (2nd Ed.)*. San Francisco: Jossey-Bass.

McKimm, J. (2009). Quality, standards and enhancement. In H. Fry, S. Ketteridge and S. Marshall (Eds.), *A handbook for teaching and learning in higher education: Enhancing academic practice. (3rd Ed.)*. New York: Routledge.

Parkes, J. and Harris, M. B. (2002). *The purposes of a syllabus. College Teaching, 50* (2), 55-61.

Three

Levels of Learning and Instructional Methods

Levels of Learning

While there are numerous theoretical models of learning (e.g., cognitive, behavioural, constructivist, developmental) the approach we take here draws from a tradition of educational research (perhaps best exemplified by the work of Bloom and colleagues in the 1950s) that considers how learning can be categorized as belonging to different domains, namely the **cognitive**, **affective** and **psychomotor** domains (Bloom et al., 1956; Krathwohl et al., 1973; Simpson, 1972).

Importantly, we do not specifically regard the use of such taxonomy as requiring a particular theoretical approach in order to proceed in practice, as one could as easily adopt a cognitivist approach as a constructivist approach with such taxonomy. What we do stress is that **utilizing taxonomy of learning** can assist when constructing and evaluating learning outcomes, teaching methods, and assessment practices, by providing a means by which one can describe *what* **is to be learnt and** *how* **it is to be learnt.**

In addition, it may provide a means by which particular learning contexts (i.e., as involving teaching methods, forms of assessment, and feedback procedures) can be assessed for their suitability for a given learning outcome. We provide some concrete examples of this in the assessment section of this Handbook.

Many approaches to levels (or styles) of learning utilize the highly influential conceptualization of **surface** and **deep** approaches to learning (Marton and Säljö, 1976). While this model has been the focus of considerable debate within the educational literature (e.g., Howie and Bagnall, 2013), we present it here in order to provide a contextual framework that might illustrate the pitfalls associated with assuming that quality teaching and learning will automatically occur – that one need not consider the specific and contextually relevant motivations, needs or task requirements of both instructors or learners.

Surface Approach

Surface learning can be characterized as an approach that involves the non-critical or reflective acceptance of information and memorization of isolated and unlinked facts. One way of describing this approach is that it involves **information reproducing**. In short, it leads to superficial retention of material rather than developed understanding or long-term retention.

This approach can be characterized as involving task completion with a minimal level of engagement. This should not be taken as a dispositional attribute of a student, but rather reflects an outcome that is the product of particular conditions of teaching.

Deep Approach

Deep learning involves critical analysis of new information and ideas and promotes a more developed understanding and problem solving approach than surface learning. One description of this approach is that it is **knowledge transforming,** rather than simply information reproducing as with the surface approach.

This approach can be characterized as involving high levels of engagement with course material, such that a student does not merely seek to complete task requirements as quickly as possible. Again, this is not to be understood as a dispositional attribute of a student but reflects interactions occurring in a given learning environment.

Another way of conceptualizing learning is termed the **strategic approach** which has been shown to relate to student achievement motivation (Fry, Ketteridge and Marshall, 2009). This approach incorporates both surface and deep approaches in that students who are motivated to obtain high grades will strategically employ either a surface or deep approach, depending on the course requirements (e.g., types of assessments, instructional methods used).

The following table (see Table 3.1) provides a sample of factors that may be associated with why students may adopt either a surface or deep approach, and also how the teaching context may promote a particular approach (adapted from Biggs and Tang, 2007; Ramsden, 2003).

While students may employ both approaches utilizing a strategic approach, depending on task requirements and available resources, the aim of educators

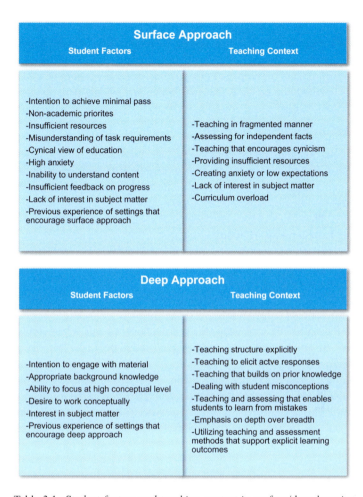

Table 3.1 *Student factors and teaching context in surface/deep learning.*

and instructors should be to ensure that instructional methods, assessment tasks, and the desired learning outcomes are aligned to ensure the best possible chance that deep learning approaches will be utilized.

Instructional Methods

In this section we will first define instructional methods. We will then turn to discussing two broad categories of instructional methods. We will then consider a more detailed description of a number of commonly utilized instructional methods. In the final sections we will examine the process of selecting the instructional method (or methods) that will best assist learners in your class and how to select employ methods that may encourage student participation.

What Are Instructional Methods?

Instructional methods are various techniques for **informing** (e.g., providing information about topics, methods, literatures related to learning outcomes) and various opportunities for **practice** (e.g., performing activities related to learning outcomes).

Types of Instructional Methods

Instructional methods may be classified into two categories (see Figure 3.1):
    1) **instructor-centred** approaches; and
    2) **learner-centred** approaches.

Instructor-centred approaches are those methods of instruction where the instructor assumes the leadership. In such methods the role of the instructor is to present the information that is to be learned and to direct the learning process of students.

    The instructor identifies the lesson objectives and takes the primary responsibility for guiding the instruction by explanation of the information and modelling. This is followed by student practice. Methods that fall under the category of the instructor-centred approaches include lecture, tutorials, field-

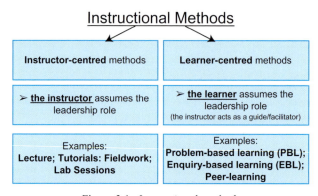

Figure 3.1 *Instructional methods.*

work and laboratory sessions.

Learner-centred approaches are those methods of instruction that enable learners to assume the leadership role in the process of their learning. The instructor in learner-centred approaches acts as a guide or facilitator. Examples of learner centred methods include problem-based learning (PBL), enquiry-based learning (EBL) and peer learning.

Rather than provide an exhaustive list of instructional methods here, we will consider some of the more widely utilized approaches and provide some suggestions for how they might best be utilized to promote student learning.

- **Instructor-Centred Methods**

Lectures

Lectures may involve traditional expository teaching (i.e., oral presentations with minimal student feedback or participation) and more interactive formats that involve student questions or demonstrations. Lectures are usually the setting in which informing is provided. Note that lectures might be conducted face-to-face or online (e.g., MOOCs), and can occur in real-time or involve pre-recorded presentations.

Tutorials

Tutorials are generally designed to be complimentary to lectures and enable more interactive approaches to material. To be effective, they require considerable preparation to ensure that there is a clear structure to the tutorial activities, which can range from question-answer interactions, demonstrations, group activities, guided reading, role-play, and modelling. While tutorials are often a setting in which informing is provided they can also be utilized as a setting in which students can be provided with opportunities for practice.

Workshops/Seminars

While similar in general form to tutorials, workshops and seminars are generally characterized by a higher degree of student led activities. If these activities involve a good blend of instruction, practical demonstrations, opportunities for hands-on practice, and a mix of instructor and peer feedback they can be very effective in providing opportunities for students to achieve learning outcomes.

However, it is important to provide **clear goals and structure** to avoid having students act as poorly trained and inexperienced instructors for other students.

Lab Sessions

In the social sciences these are often called workshops and involve practical demonstrations and enactments on such things as computer software applications, statistical procedures, video and imaging equipment, and can also involve language training and a variety of simulations. At the early skill level these will feature considerable informing and demonstrating on the part of instructors, although as students acquire higher levels of skill more emphasis can be directed towards peer instruction and feedback.

Fieldwork
The term fieldwork can be applied to any learning activities that occur outside the traditional physical academic setting, for example this might involve community based observation and research, guided excursions, attendance of events and cultural exchange settings.

Fieldwork requires the **active involvement of an instructor** to ensure that there is an appropriate structure in place to furnish information or activities related to particular learning outcomes. In short, the experiential aspects of undertaking fieldwork alone will not necessarily lead to students achieving learning outcomes – the fieldwork activities need to be selected to compliment, rather than replace, structured learning activities.

- **Learner-Centred Methods**

Problem Based Learning

> 'The problem, or a series of problems, is where learning starts, and in going about solving those problems the learner seeks out the necessary knowledge of disciplines, facts and procedures.' (Biggs and Tang, 2007)

Simply stated, this is a method that involves the instructor presenting the student with a problem that must be solved. In short, with problem based learning (PBL) it is the problems that define what is to be learned. This approach is often utilized in applied science courses and courses in which professional skills are taught and evaluated, and more often at the postgraduate level. Indeed, a research higher degree with minimal coursework could be regarded as an exemplar of PBL.

However, PBL can be effectively utilized at the undergraduate level provided sufficient care and attention is directed towards matching desired learning outcomes with appropriate problems, and that sufficient resources are available for learning support, feedback, and time for completion of assessments.

Assessments here should be performance based, and thus require instructors to be able to provide enough learning opportunities for students to have a reasonable chance of obtaining the performance based learning outcomes.

The goals of PBL are:
- Structuring knowledge for use in working contexts (PBL is concerned with constructing knowledge that is to be put to work).
- Developing effective reasoning processes.
- Developing self-directed learning skills.
- Increased motivation for learning.
- Developing group skills, working with colleagues.

Enquiry Based Learning (EBL)
This approach to teaching and learning draws upon the previously described range of instructional methods, however the main focus is placed on having a process of enquiry that is driven and directed by students.

What EBL can involve:

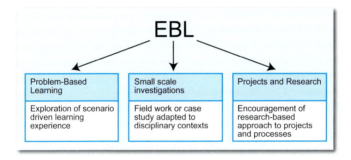

Figure 3.2 *EBL examples.*[1]

- Students (rather than instructors) drive the learning process.
- Emphasis is on small group work and the use of use of a wide range of information resources.
- Instructors act as facilitators rather than all-knowing experts, and provide encouragement and support to student projects.
- Students may formulate their own research topics and convert that research into useful knowledge.
- Students gain a range of transferable skills through this process that involve

---

1) Centre for Excellence in Enquiry-Based Learning, Manchester University. http://www.campus.manchester.ac.uk/ceebl/ebl/

both academic and practical domains of knowledge.

The Problem Solving Approach

Documented problem solving is a classroom assessment technique that assists instructors in understanding students' problem-solving strategies. It is a flexible tool that can be applied to a variety of disciplines.

Why this Approach?
- It requires students to think about how they approach a problem as they write down the solution steps.
- It connects the student's reflection on the thought process and the instructor's ability to essentially view the thought process.
- Insight into the learning process is beneficial since it allows students and instructors to address learning gaps.
- It also establishes a dialog with individual students about their learning. This is especially helpful when students are too shy or lack the self-confidence to ask questions during class.
- It measures student understanding on a more frequent basis than exams alone.

How to Implement?
- **As part of a homework assignment**
  Students complete the solution individually and outside of class. Instructors can identify a specific homework question and require students to document it.
- **As an individual in-class activity**
  Students, working individually, write the solution which provides *real time assessment* for both students and the instructor. This can be done spontaneously by pausing during a lecture.
- **As a collaborative in-class activity**
  Students work together in groups of 2 or 3 to produce the solution; the instructor can walk around the room and encourage students to interact.
- **As part of a simulation or game**
  Students are provided with background information necessary for simulation or game participation (with or without clearly defined objectives or end goals) and the instructor acts as facilitator.

Three Essential Steps
1. **Introduce the process in class**
   Pose a question or problem and ask students to indicate the steps required to answer it.
2. **Provide incentives for student participation**
   Tie it to a homework assignment or offer an extra credit (should be mentioned in the syllabus as class participation)
3. **Provide feedback to students on their solution process**
   A written response to each student, noting steps that were missed and any terms that were misused.

Documented Problem Solving (DPS)
An active learning strategy and a classroom assessment technique that requires students to formulate the steps they use in order to solve a problem or answer a question, including all the steps.

- The steps should include what students are thinking as they go through the process.
- Solutions are written in complete sentences.
- May be hand written or typed but must be legible.
- Must be submitted on notebook paper or letter size paper.

For students, the goal is to improve learning and enhance the retention of knowledge. It also helps identify missteps made by students. Plus, as a result of this activity, students should become more aware of their own critical thinking and problem-solving strategies. This awareness can be transferred to other coursework.

In addition, this method allows the instructor to become more aware of how students address problems and more knowledgeable about student misconceptions. This gives the instructor the opportunity to readdress concepts that are unclear prior to an exam. Finally, by providing feedback on the DPS, the instructor has an opportunity to communicate with students in a very direct manner.

Peer-Learning
Peer learning can involve a range of **student-directed activities**, for example student study partners, group based work, peer teaching, and so forth. This can take place in face-to-face settings or be conducted online (or a utilize a mix of both).

While this type of learning usually takes place as a component of one of the other methods previously described, it can be useful to conceptualize it as a discrete method.

Rather than assuming that peer learning will automatically take place with a given instructional methods or strategy (e.g., tutorials) **the context and form in which the peer learning can be facilitated should be given careful consideration.**

Instructors may wish to provide students with feedback regularly and ask other students to provide feedback as well. Benefits for students may include (Chalmers and Kelly, 1997):

- A friendly environment in which students can comfortably ask 'the dumbest questions'.
- Weekly study that keeps them up to date.
- Insight into the range of material other students are covering and the difficulties they have.
- A mentor who can give information and who has inside knowledge of how they coped.
- International students particularly like the opportunity to discuss without staff present.

Self-Directed Learning

This can include a wide range of activities including individual reading, project work, reflective diary construction, portfolio work, and what are usually referred to as generic study skills (i.e., critical reading, writing, literature reviewing and library skills). Again, like peer learning practices it is important not to assume that self-directed learning will automatically take place as the result of engagement with other instructional methods.

Opportunities for self-directed learning need to be carefully planned, and students may require considerable support in order that they understand how to successfully undertake self-learning activities.

Case Studies
Case studies are traditionally associated with social science classes, but can be used in any discipline in which students need to explore how issues and principles learned in class interact in real world situations.

Typically, a case study has three common elements:
1. **Real-World Scenario**
   Cases are generally based on real world situations, although some facts may be changed to simplify the scenario or to protect privacy.
2. **Supporting Data and Documents**
   Effective cases assignments typically provide real world artefacts for students to analyse. These can be simple data tables, links to websites, images, video, or appropriate material.
3. **Open-Ended Problem**
   Most case assignments require students to answer an open-ended question or develop a solution to an open-ended problem with multiple potential solutions.

Case assignments can be done in *teams or independently*. Typically, cases are done in teams so that the students can brainstorm solutions and share the work load.

Benefits of Case Studies
Many courses use case studies in their curriculum to teach content, involve students with real life data or provide opportunities for students to put themselves in the decision maker's shoes. Some of the primary benefits include:
1. **Real World Context**
   Not only do students see how the course material applies to the world outside the classroom, but they get to see how data is often ambiguous or not clearly defined in many situations.
2. **Explore Multiple Perspectives**
   Cases in which a decision is required can be used to expose students to viewpoints from multiple sources and see why people may want different outcomes. Students can see how a decision will impact different participants, both positively and negatively.
3. **Requires Critical Thinking and Analysis**
   Cases usually require students to analyse data in order to reach a conclusion. Since many assignments are open-ended, students can practice choosing appropriate analytic techniques as well.
4. **Students Synthesize Course Content**
   Many cases require students to pull in different analytic techniques and information from different areas of the course in order to provide an effective solution to the problem. In addition, a case assignment can require an initial statement of the facts and techniques used to reach the conclusion.

Selecting Instructional Methods

While the number of different instructional methods may be daunting to consider when designing a new course, making prudent decisions on an overall teaching strategy that considers how teaching can be aligned with learning outcomes, assessment methods, and feedback provision is likely to yield best practice.

- Is the teaching method likely to support students achieving the specified learning outcomes?
- Is the teaching method likely to provide opportunities for student and instructor feedback?
- Is there a good balance between providing informing and opportunities for practice?
- Are the methods justified in terms of the resources required (i.e., time, equipment, personnel, workload) to provide support for students achieving the specified learning outcomes?
- Are there better alternatives available that may promote deep learning?

The following (Figure 3.3) may assist in the selection of relevant teaching methods and learning activities that may provide for learning activities (adapted from Biggs and Tag, 2007).

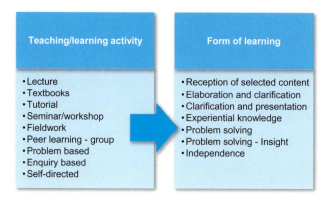

Figure 3.3 *Learning activities and forms of learning.*

While this may assist with thinking about the *form* of learning that might be best suited for a particular learning outcome, another useful strategy is to

3 Levels of Learning and Instructional Methods

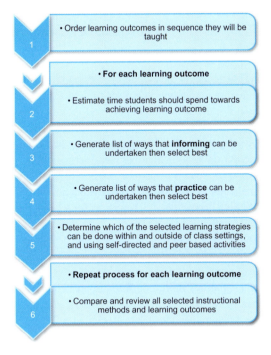

Figure 3.4 *Constructing learning outcomes.*

consider the learning outcomes first and then generate ways in which those outcomes can best be achieved. In short, the initial focus should be toward what you intend students to achieve at the completion of your course (in terms of skills and knowledge) rather than how you will be teaching. For each course, order the learning outcomes in the sequence they will be taught, and for each learning outcome consider the following (Figure 3.4):

Encouraging Class Participation

Class participation is an integral part of instructional methods and it is important beyond grades. However, grading class participation signals students about their growth in critical thinking, active learning, development of listening and speaking skills needed for career success, and the ability to join a discipline's conversation. Actively involving students in class activities that require them to discuss readings, apply concepts and practice what they are learning will lead to better student learning outcomes (Davis, 2009).

55

Guidelines that can be Used to Promote Class Participation
1. State it clearly in your syllabus, establish it as an expectation at the first day of class.
2. Count it as part of the grade.
3. Sit among the students during the discussion part of the class.
4. If one student is dominating the discussion at the expense of the others – break eye contact with that student and look at others.

Difficulties in Grading Class Participation (Jacobs and Chase, 1992)
1. No instruction on how to improve class participation.
2. Interpretation of student behaviour is often difficult and subjective.
3. Disadvantageous for shy or introverted students.
4. Record-keeping is problematic, so grades for a given individual are hard to justify if challenged.

Strategies to Overcome the Grading Problem with Class Participation
- Create activities in which students report on homework already prepared
 Often, quiet people are more comfortable speaking in class if they can prepare ahead of time.
- Include an Email Component for Class Participation
 Many students who are pathologically quiet in class come to life through

Grade	Criteria
0	• Absent in more than 10 % of the classes
1	• Tries to respond when called on but does not offer much • Demonstrates very infrequent involvement in discussion
2	• Demonstrates adequate preparation but sporadic involvement • Offers straightforward information without elaboration
3	• Demonstrates good preparation • Offers interpretations and analysis of the study material • Contributes well to discussion in an on-going way: responds to other students' points, thinks through own points • Demonstrates consistent on-going involvement
4	• Demonstrates excellent preparation • Offers analysis, synthesis, and evaluation of study material, e.g., puts together pieces of the discussion to develop new approaches that take the class further. • Contributes in a very significant way to on-going discussion • Demonstrates on-going very active involvement

Table 3.2 *Example of grading class participation.*

email.
- Increase Wait Time
  A level playing field method in classroom participation is to pose a question and then to enforce a minute or so of silence for students to structure their reply.
- Coach Problematic Students and Reward Progress

Instructors can also invite students who are not successfully participating in class to an office conference where the instructor can speak honestly about the problem and listen to students perspectives and concerns

Example of Grading Class Participation
To evaluate participation in the class a good starting point is to develop a set of behavioural indicators of good performance suitable for a subject. Behavioural indicators could be a combination of both objective (such as absence) and subjective (such as positive outlook, enthusiasm, etc.). In Table 3.2, we demonstrate a set of evaluation criteria. It is important to give it to students at the beginning of the semester so they know which behaviours will be rewarded with high participation grades. In Table 3.2 the expectations for class participation is summarized on a scale from 0 (lowest) through 4 (highest).

References
Biggs, J. and Tang, C. (2007). *Teaching for quality learning at university (3rd Ed.)*. Maidenhead: Open University Press/McGraw Hill.
Bloom, B.S., Engelhart, M.D., Furst, E.J., Hill, W.H. and Krathwohl, D.R. (Eds.). (1956). *Taxonomy of educational objectives: The classification of educational goals. Handbook I: Cognitive domain*. New York: McKay.
Chalmers, D. and Kelly, B. (1997). *Peer Assisted Study Sessions (PASS)*. University of Queensland, Teaching and Educational Development Institute.
Davis, B.G. (2009). *Tools for teaching (2nd Ed.)*. San Francisco: Jossey-Bass.
Fry, H., Ketteridge, S. and Marshall, S. (Eds.). (2009). *A handbook for teaching and learning in higher education: Enhancing academic practice. (3rd Ed.)*. New York:. Routledge.
Howie, P. and Bagnall, R. (2013). A critique of the deep and surface approaches to learning model. *Teaching in Higher Education, 18*(4), 389-400.
Jacobs, L.C. and Chase, C. (1992). *Developing and using tests effectively: a guide for faculty*. San Francisco: Jossey-Bass.
Krathwohl, D.R., Bloom, B.S., and Masia, B.B. (1973). *Taxonomy of educational objectives, the classification of educational goals, handbook II: affective domain*. New York: McKay.
Marton, F. and Säljö, R. (1976). On qualitative differences in learning. I – Outcome

and Process. *British Journal of Educational Psychology 46*, 4-11.

Ramsden, P. (2003). *Learning to teach in higher education (2nd Ed.)*. London: Routledge

Simpson, E.J. (1972). *The classification of educational objectives in the psychomotor domain.* Washington: Gryphon House.

Four

Assessment as Linked-up Practice

It is important to consider that assessment (i.e., the measuring and reporting of student achievement of specified learning outcomes) should be considered as a component of an overall teaching and learning strategy. Rather than merely appending some form of assessment to a program of teaching it is profitable to consider that assessment is itself part of the learning process. We strongly advocate the use of **criterion-referenced grading** for evaluating assessments, which involves measuring and reporting student achievement against a predefined benchmark (i.e., a set of **learning outcomes**). The use of such standards based systems is becoming widespread in international higher education contexts, as it emphasizes individual student learning and mastery of course materials rather than simply assessing student performance compared to other students. For example, assigning grades on the basis of arbitrary cut-off points or using predetermined distributions of scores (Waugh and Gronlund, 2012).

Principles of Effective Assessment (Brown, 2001)

- Assessment guides learning (i.e., learning outcomes specify what is to be taught, and how it is to be assessed) so if an educator requires changes in learning then changing the assessment method is required.
- Match assessment tasks to learning outcomes.
- Match criteria to the task and learning outcomes.
- Keep criteria simple.
- Be fair, reliable, and valid in marking.
- Provide meaningful and timely feedback.

Forms of Assessment

Broadly, we can conceive of assessment as involving two distinct forms in contemporary higher education settings, being **formative** or **summative** (Juwah et al., 2004).

Formative Assessment

Formative assessment is used to identify issues in performance and attainment of knowledge and skills, and is usually undertaken as part of an on-going teaching process. This form of assessment does not require formal testing and any assessment is usually provided for feedback purposes. Examples of formative assessment include weekly quizzes, short answer tests, reflective diaries, and class discussions and presentations. Formative feedback need not be restricted to instructors providing feedback to students, in many assessment contexts peers provide useful formative feedback. The focus of formative assessment should be towards providing students with opportunities for constructive feedback on their performance, in addition to providing instructors an opportunity to monitor and evaluate the effectiveness of teaching.

Summative Assessment

This form of assessment involves the formal testing and evaluation of knowledge and skills that have been specified as learning outcomes, and generally involves the awarding of marks and grades. While emphasis is often placed mainly on the development and implementation of summative assessment, utilizing both forms of assessment can produce more effective measures of performance.

Regardless of the assessment method utilized, it is important that care should be directed towards ensuring that assessments are constructed and reviewed to ensure both the **validity** of assessments (i.e., the appropriateness of the assessment for a given purpose) and the **reliability** of assessments (i.e., that assessments will produce comparable results across students and instructors).

In other words, it is important that comparable work is given the same assessment, regardless of when, who or where the grading takes place. This is not only an issue of fairness and accountability, but it also has very real consequences when the grades that students receive may impact on scholarship, exchange, graduate-degree and employment opportunities.

Assessment Methods[1]

When considering the type (and number) of assessments that should be undertaken in a given course, it is important that a wide range of methods should be employed whenever possible. This maximizes potential validity, provides opportunities for formative feedback, and allows for a range of learning styles to be accommodated.

The following is not provided as an exhaustive list of all possible forms of assessment, but rather to provide some quick notes on potential advantages and disadvantages of a range of assessment methods and strategies. In addition, we would strongly encourage that the development and implementation of specific teaching methods in a given course of study should take place alongside assessment planning.

- **Multiple choice questions (MCQ)**

One of the most widely used forms of assessment, this assessment method requires students to select a correct answer from a limited number of alternatives. MCQs can employ a variety of question and response formats. One major advantage of MCQ is that a wide range of knowledge can be quickly sampled. MCQ can be utilized to measure understanding, analysis, problem solving, and evaluative skills. While more complex formats can be utilized, this may entail a risk that students may find them unnecessarily confusing. Another risk is that poor question design can lead to the testing of relatively trivial knowledge. While they may be difficult and time consuming to construct, they are generally easy to score and analyse. MCQs may also be useful for self-assessment and screening. Feedback, in the form of numbers of correct or incorrect responses, can be given to students quickly – although detailed feedback may require considerable work. Multiple assessors can produce useful question items quickly when utilizing learning outcomes to structure questions.

- **Short answer questions**

This method is useful in measuring analysis, the application of knowledge, and problem-solving and evaluative skills. One particular advantage is that they are easier to design than complex MCQs. Having model answers to assist in the

---

[1] This section draws extensively from: Angelo, T. and Cross, K. (1993). *Classroom assessment techniques: A handbook for college teachers (2nd Ed.)*. San Francisco: Jossey-Bass; Brown, G. (2001). *Assessment: A guide for lecturers*. York. LTSN Generic Centre; and Bryan, C. and Clegg, K. (2006). *Innovative assessment in higher education*. London: Routledge.

marking process provides for a relatively fast process compared with some other forms of assessment (e.g., problems, essays, projects) but is usually considerably more time consuming than marking MCQs.

- **Single essay examination**

This form of assessment involves students preparing for a selected topic (or topics) and constructing a written essay within a time limit (usually 2-3 hours in a UK context). Essay examinations are relatively easy to design; however attention should be directed towards both learning and assessment criteria. One major advantage of this form of assessment is that a wide range of learning outcomes can be examined, including (for example) the capacity to draw on a wide range of knowledge, and to synthesize and identify recurrent themes. One disadvantage is that marking for feedback purposes can be relatively slow, although marking for grading can be fast with the use of simple criteria.

- **Essays**

While essays are perhaps the most common assessment method utilized in higher education (along with MCQs and short answer questions) it is important to recognize that different types of essays will test different styles of writing and types of thinking. Essays can measure skills such as understanding, synthesis, and evaluation, providing care is directed towards constructing appropriate questions. Essays have a number of advantages, including the ease by which they can be structured to assess specific course learning outcomes. However, one obvious disadvantage is they can be very time consuming when marking to be provide explicit feedback. Another potential disadvantage is that variations between (and within) markers can be considerable, and it is important to ensure simple criteria are employed to minimize variability in marking. Finally, where class members are not English L1 learners this kind of assessment can place a heavy burden on students.

- **Oral examinations**

Oral examinations (i.e., conducted between single students and examiners) can test a number of skills such as communication, understanding, procedural knowledge, and practical skills. In addition, they can provide a useful context in which relatively direct feedback on performance can be provided. However, it is important that examiners utilize clear protocols to ensure consistency – both in terms of intra- and inter-examiner reliability.

- **Presentations**

Utilizing student presentations (to either an instructor or to peers) can be an effective way of assessing a wide range of skills. One advantage in utilizing presentations is that marking for grading utilizing simple criteria is fast and potentially reliable. In addition, presentations provide for additional measures of ability, for example ability to respond to questions and possibly deal with challenges and conflict. As with oral examinations, they provide a useful context in which feedback can be provided, potentially from multiple sources. When assessing group presentations, while marking and feedback can be undertaken quickly, care should be directed to ensuring that individual versus group performance is taken into account. It should also be noted that for students watching their peer's presenting, unless active listening activities are included, the activity is passive and results in little learning. Thus, while assessing student presentations it is important to also think about the learning process for the students who become the audience of that presentation. Carefully designed learning activities can enhance the satisfaction of students with this form of assessment.

- **Problem Setting**

This form of assessment involves setting specific problems for students to solve. They may be problems that have discrete (and a priori) model solutions, or can require open-ended or on-going investigations. This type of assessment can measure skills relating to the application, analysis, and engagement with problem solving strategies. Some disadvantages are that complex problems and associated marking criteria can be difficult to design, and that marking and providing feedback of complex problems can be difficult. Advantages are that marking for grading of easy problems is fast, and that variability in marking is low when using model solutions/answers or well-designed marking criteria.

- **Practical reports**

This form of assessment generally involves the provision of a report following from a course of "hands on" instruction (e.g., lab report, case study). Reports can be useful in measuring knowledge of experimental procedures, data collection methods, and the analysis and interpretation of results. While reports can be utilized with practical and performance based skills (e.g., interviewing) it is important to consider that these will only assess knowledge of practice/performance and not ability with the practical skills themselves. Marking for grading and feedback can be fast when utilizing structured forms. One potential disadvantage of this form of assessment is that variation between markers can be high. Another type of practical report involves delivering a practice based session, which might involve students demonstrating a range of skills and knowledge in practical application. This may also be undertaken under timed conditions, and can involve peer feedback or assessing. While practical sessions may provide for high levels of ecological validity (and may be useful in clinical or applied courses) they are often time consuming and require considerable planning. In addition training may be required when using multiple assessors to ensure reliability of evaluations and assessments.

- **Modified essay questions**

While similar to the use of essay questions, in this assessment method a sequence of questions is constructed that are focused on a specific theme or topic. This may also involve a single case study (and is often referred to as a '*interrupted case study*'). Following the provision of an answer to the first question, students are presented with additional information and a further question or opportunity to request additional information. This procedure continues until questions are exhausted, or a time limit is reached. While constructing and delivering this form of assessment can be challenging depending on the material to be examined, major advantages are that there is usually a high degree of practical utility, particularly when 'real world' scenarios or case studies are utilized.

- **Poster sessions**

Utilizing poster sessions (which are often conducted like mini-conference sessions) can test skills such as the capacity to present findings and interpretations succinctly and attractively. However, one risk is that too much emphasis can be placed on presentation methods while overlooking other skills and abilities. Advantages are that marking and feedback can be provided quickly, and that feedback can be from multiple sources (i.e., instructor, peers, and self). When assessing group poster sessions, while marking and feedback can be undertaken quickly, care should be directed to ensuring that individual versus group performance is taken into account. Utilizing simple and clear criteria is important to minimize variability of marking.

- **Direct observation**

Direct observation of student performance can be useful in estimating performance and providing immediate feedback. This may be particularly useful in clinical settings or in settings in which the instructor is required to adopt an active participation role. This form of assessment can also involve peer observation or performance. Advantages of this method are that reliability and validity can be high when utilizing structured observation. However, training is required for high reliability if detailed checklists or protocols are used.

- **Learning logs/reflective diaries**

The use of learning logs and learning diaries can involve a wide variety of formats, including structured questionnaires or forms, chronological accounts of practices, or more free ranging reflective accounts. It is important that logs or diaries are aligned with specific learning outcomes, as they can lack focus or represent work that is not directly related to the teaching and learning outcomes of a given course. In addition, they can require considerable work both in terms of their production and assessing, so it is important that a framework is employed that clearly specifies the role of the task in terms of assessment and evaluation of learning.

- **Portfolios**

This form of assessment involves students compiling an archive, which may involve a wide range of media. The archive may feature textual materials, but can also include internet based materials, artwork or other media. It is important that portfolio are aligned with specific learning outcomes; as with learning logs or reflective diaries they can lack focus or represent work that is not directly related to the teaching and learning outcomes of a given course. The use of portfolio requires the instructor to provide a clear framework for what should be included in the portfolio, and clear rationale provided on how the portfolio will be assessed.

- **Projects, group projects, and dissertations**

Projects can involve a wide range of topics, themes, and practical activities and can effectively assess a wide range of practical, analytical, and interpretative skills. In addition, projects may provide for broader assessments of a wider application of knowledge, understanding, and skills related to real or simulated situations. The use of project based assessment may also provide a measure of time management skills, and utilizing group projects can provide a measure of teamwork and leadership skills. One of the biggest advantages of project-based assessments is the broad scope of skills and abilities that can be tested, both in terms of specific and more general skills. One significant disadvantage with using project based assessment, in settings in which students are undertaking a range of projects within a given course, is that the variability in project topics may make it difficult to grade projects fairly. However, the use of clear criteria can reduce variability in marking.

- **Case studies and scenarios**

The use of case studies involves students investigating and reporting on potential solutions or developing analytic insights into specific features of a case, can be useful in measuring the application of knowledge, problem-solving, and evaluative skills. Cases from 'real world' situations are often used, particularly in courses that stress practical application of knowledge and skills. Alternatively, cases can be designed specifically in order to promote analytic skills rather than applied skills. While brief case studies are easy to design, implement and assess, more complex cases may require considerable time and effort to develop and implement.

- **Computer-based assessment**

A form of assessment that is becoming widely utilized is e-learning platforms, often featuring multiple choice question examinations or short answer essay questions. While generally utilized to assess individual students, novel approaches to computer-based assessment can involve collaborative, online problem solving or group collaboration (e.g., construction of wiki, blog or other online resource).

- **Simulated interviews**

Simulated interviews can be useful for assessing oral communication skills and for developing ways of giving and receiving feedback on performance. These can be audio or video-recorded and utilized for self and peer based assessment. These may feature in clinical or applied coursework, but can also be utilized in simulations or role-plays.

- **Reflective practice assignments**

This generally involves students undertaking some practical activities while maintaining a reflective journal or log of their experiences. Reflective practice assignments can allow for the measurement of analysis and evaluative experiences, particularly when these are framed in the context of relevant theoretical and conceptual literatures.

- **Work based assessment**

This type of assessment involves fieldwork or work placement (i.e., internships) and utilizes a variety of methods, including learning logs, portfolios, projects, and structured reports from supervisors or mentors. It is important to provide supervisors and mentors training in the use of criteria prior to any training or assessment experience. One of the major disadvantages is that given work experiences can be diverse it may be problematic to ensure adequate reliability of assessment against criteria, and difficult to establish clear linkages between learning outcomes and work based experiences.

- **Simulations and games**

This form of assessment can involve the use of complex, 'real world' simulations, or more abstract game scenarios. For example, a simulation could involve the development of briefing materials based on real world events or situations, and students are given various roles in which they attempt to develop processes, solutions or other outcomes relevant to the desired learning outcomes. Simulations and games can involve a wide variety of learning objectives and outcomes, in which both the acquisition and application of relevant knowledge and skills can be assessed, however this may require considerable skill to develop and implement effectively. The use of simulations of games requires considerable preparation by an instructor, and may require several assessors if the simulation or game is designed to provide students with opportunities to be assessed across multiple tasks within a given setting.

Selecting Assessment Strategies

Given the range of potential assessment methods that can be employed it is important to consider what kinds of methods are best suited to assessing the key learning outcomes of a particular course. One strategy is that for each course, consider the specified learning outcomes in turn and match them with an appropriate assessment method.

The final goal of any assessment selection and design should be to aim for the following:
- Assessment methods are aligned with learning outcomes.
- Assessment weightings are appropriate (in terms of time and resources required) given the importance of specific learning outcomes.
- Assessment methods are distributed evenly over the duration of a course.
- Assessment methods are selected from a range of methods.
- Assessment criteria are clear and can be communicated to students.
- Assessment methods and criteria fit the cultural context of the classroom and the level/range of language proficiency.

Summary

Regardless of the form of assessment, the assessment should have clear learning outcomes specified and these should be linked to the overall course learning outcomes. Students should be provided with a copy of the assessment requirements.

Criteria and Descriptors

While assigning numerical scores to work or fitting scores within specified grade bands may assist when attempting to rank order student performance, this does not provide any real measure of how performance relates to specified learning outcomes. In this regard, it is important to ensure that marking and evaluation is linked to specific assessment criteria and associated descriptors. Often there are several criteria that are employed for any single piece of assessable work.

For example, a written essay may have criteria relating to the introduction, the conclusion, the references, and general presentation. Each of these criteria may be scored in a range that characterizes a specific level of performance, using various descriptors of performance.

Types of Criteria[2]

- **Intuitive:** Here the criteria are implicit in the work required. Examiners use his or her intuition to judge the quality of the work. One of the major disadvantages with using implicit criteria is that they remain hidden from other markers and students and can thus pose problems for establishing reliable and valid grading.
- **Global:** The criteria are based on key features of the work, for example organization and evidence of reading. The assessment leads directly to a single mark. An advantage with using global criteria is that marking can be fast and reliability high. One disadvantage is that providing feedback to students can be slow.
- **Criterion reference grading:** This represents the use of general criteria for grading students' work. One advantage of criterion reference grading is that marking can be fast and feedback to students is fairly fast.
- **Broad criteria:** These are criteria that are based on ratings or marks. These are most often utilized to assess qualities that permeate the whole of an assessment task such as fluency of style or organization. Usually reliable and feedback can be fast if based on the criteria.
- **Specific criteria:** While these can provide more detail than broad criteria one major disadvantage is that they can overlap and the meaning of each of the criteria can be unclear. Additionally, they can be burdensome to use, variations between markers on specific criteria can be low, and while feed-

---

2) Adapted from Brown, G. (2001). *Assessment: A guide for lecturers.* York. LTSN Generic Centre.

back to students can be fast it might not be necessarily useful.
- **Marking schemes:** These are often used for linear marking such as specific subject content, operations or procedures, or an accurate translation of a paragraph in a passage of prose. One disadvantage is that they can be time consuming to complete, particularly with work that has systemic problems. One major advantage is that they usually promote high reliability and validity.
- **Checklists:** These can be employed to assess sequential tasks and simple design specifications. One disadvantage is that they may be time consuming when assessing complex tasks, although they generally have good reliability.
- **Detailed checklists:** Utilizing more detailed checklists can improve validity but not necessarily reliability. In addition, these may be more time consuming and difficult to use. Not necessarily helpful as a feedback tool for students if qualitative feedback additional to checklist items is not provided.
- **Detailed criteria:** Probably the least reliable method and most time-consuming instrument of assessment.

Assessment descriptors are qualitative evaluations that link the numeric grade/band with a description of performance. Such descriptors serve not only as useful benchmarks in the evaluation and grading of work, but also serve to provide feedback on performance to students.

Biggs (2003, p. 54) provides a useful procedure for developing qualitative descriptors (Figure 4.1).

Figure 4.1 *Developing qualitative descriptors (Biggs, 2003, p.54).*

It can be useful to think of constructing descriptors with various performance and achievement verbs, for example the following (which can be considered to represent the previously discussed cognitive, affective, and psychomotor domains) can be used in the construction of assessment descriptors.

Cognitive Domain[3]

Knowing

define	label	identify
relate	distinguish	memorize
recall	list	recognize

Understanding

classify	review	restate	generalize
explain	report	organize	demonstrate
identify	illustrate	estimate	model
interpret	apply	apply	simulate

Thinking

analyse	propose	categorize	justify
produce	develop	criticize	rate
appraise	argue	deduce	contrast
solve	assess	formulate	compare
evaluate	synthesize	judge	contrast

Affective Domain[4]

Receiving

listen to	awareness of	alert to	sensitive to
show tolerance	reply	answer	follow
approve			

---

3) Adapted from LaSere Erickson, B. and Weltner Strommer, D. (1991). *Teaching College Freshman.* San Francisco: Jossey Bass.

4) Adapted from Krathwohl.D.R., Bloom, B.S., and Masia, B.B. (1969).*A taxonomy of educational objectives, the classification of educational goals, handbook II: affective domain.* New York: McKay.

Valuing

accept	attain	assume	support
participate	continue	grow	

Behaviour

organize	select	judge	decide
identify	develop	consider	
practice	continues	undertakes	incorporates

Psychomotor Domain[5]

Perception

detect	differentiate	distinguish	identify
observe	isolate	associate	compare

Adaptation

adapt	modify	change	adjust
integrate	revise	combine	convert

Origination

originate	create	devise	compose
construct	design	formulate	develop

Descriptors

The following brief lists of descriptors are adjectives that can be used to describe levels of performance.

Low level of performance

wrong	incomplete	incorrect	unstructured
limited	inconsistent	missing	confusing

---

5) Adapted from Simpson, E.J. (1972). *The classification of educational objectives in the psychomotor domain.* Washington: Gryphon House.

Moderate level of performance

satisfactory	careful	coherent	confident
descriptive	structured	accurate	adequate

High level of performance

creative	authoritative	critical	persuasive
sophisticated	ambitious	original	inspiring

Using Criteria and Descriptors

After selecting assessment strategies, it is important to ensure that marking and evaluation is linked to specific assessment criteria and associated descriptors.

Just to recap, with regard to assessment, some key points to consider are that:

- Assessment should be **reliable**.
- Assessment must measure student attainment of **learning outcomes**.
- **Criteria** identify what is to be assessed.
- **Descriptors** allow us to distinguish between different levels of attainment.

An Example of Aligning Assessment with Learning Outcomes

> **Course: Critical Thinking Skills**
> **The principle aims of the course are:**
>
> - Equip students with a range of thinking and learning strategies that foster critical thinking;
> - To enable students to analyse, evaluate and generate claims;
> - To enable students to reflect and challenge their own thinking practices;
> - To enable students to appreciate the value of critical thinking skills in both academic and everyday settings.
>
> **The key course learning outcomes are that students can (upon successful course completion):**

- Identify, evaluate and construct different forms of argument and persuasion;
- Identify rhetorical devices and strategies utilized in making truth claims; • Recognize common fallacies in everyday reasoning;
- Use a range of resources, including primary research papers and information technology;
- Use evidence to support or challenge an argument;
- Demonstrate a range of transferable skills including oral and written communication, effective planning and organisation, and independence.

Sample Assignment: Critical Analysis of Editorial

For this assignment you are required to provide a brief (1,000 words) critical analysis of a newspaper editorial. The main aim of this assignment is to provide you with an opportunity to critically assess and critique a piece of text and demonstrate your awareness of common flaws and pitfalls in critical thinking.
The main focus will be on how you identify issues in critical thinking.

- ✓ Identify the main argument or claim that is being presented
- ✓ Provide analysis of the evidence the author uses to support their argument
- ✓ Identify any rhetorical devices, fallacies or other issues you think are problems with the argument.

How these are matched with the learning outcomes:
- Identify the main argument or claim that is being presented
    This is aligned with *Identify, evaluate and construct different forms of argument and persuasion.*
- Provide analysis of the evidence the author uses to support their argument
    This is aligned with *Use evidence to support or challenge an argument.*
- Identify any rhetorical devices, fallacies, or other issues you think are problems with the argument.
    This is aligned with *Identify rhetorical devices and strategies utilized in making truth claims* and *Recognize common fallacies in everyday reasoning.*

Preventing Plagiarism and Setting Internationalization Goals

Plagiarism

Defining it:
In an instructional setting, plagiarism occurs when a writer deliberately uses someone else's language, ideas, or other original (not common-knowledge) material without acknowledging its source (Council of Writing Program Administrators, 2003[6])

Steps to reduce or prevent plagiarism incidents:

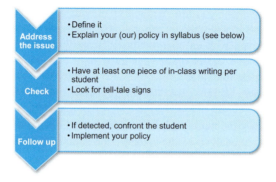

It is very important to present the plagiarism policy during the orientation and in the course syllabus to ensure that students are informed of their responsibilities in addition to ensuring they are then accountable for violations of plagiarism policies.

Example of Plagiarism Policy Statement in Course Syllabus

> **Assessment requirements**
> - Academic misconduct (cheating, collusion, plagiarism or falsification of information) in all forms of written work, lab tests, demonstrations, designs, presentations, in-class tests and examination can lead to consequences ranging from loss of marks in the relevant course to zero grades for all classes taken that semester.

---

6) http://www.wpacouncil.org/positions/WPAplagiarism.pdf

Internationalization Goals in Course Syllabi

One of the major aims of our Human Sciences International Undergraduate Degree Program is to build up in our students a sophisticated knowledge base and the necessary practical skills to meet the challenges of our fast-changing, globalized world. Our program also aims to nurture in students a high level of inter-cultural competency. To achieve these goals, internationalizing the course is very important.

How we can internationalize courses (at the course planning level):
- Include analysis of international case studies.
- Set tasks that require students to discuss, analyse, and evaluate information from a range of international sources.
- Address global, economic, political, environmental, social, ethical, health issues in course content.
- Include lectures/presentations from guest lecturers, using their international experience; or existing academic staff with overseas experience.

Final Comments

With any assessment it may be prudent to consider how the assessment fits with other assessment tasks at a comparable level, both in terms of difficulty, time required to meet learning outcomes, and format. Again, this is one way in which having an aligned curriculum can be useful. Rather than working on assessment tasks in isolation from other courses and instructors, having an aligned curriculum can afford opportunities for improving teaching and learning practices.

For example, rather than having a degree program that is comprised of numerous independent courses and assessments, with individual instructors (and students) having no clear idea of how the various courses "hang together", it can be possible to employ **clustering** of assessments. This involves developing assessment tasks that cut across several courses, or having assessment tasks that are sequentially undertaken as students progress through different course levels. The goal should be towards ensuring that every individual assessment has a clear rationale and purpose when taking into account the overall aims and objectives of the program.

References

Angelo, T. and Cross, K. (1993). *Classroom assessment techniques: A handbook for college teachers (2nd Ed.)*. San Francisco: Jossey-Bass Biggs, J. (2003). *Teaching for quality learning at university (2nd Ed.)*. Buckingham: Society for Research into Higher Education/Open University Press. p. 54.

Brown, G. (2001). *Assessment: A guide for lecturers*. York. LTSN Generic Centre. http://www.bioscience.heacademy.ac.uk/ftp/Resources/gc/assess03Lecturers.pdf

Bryan, C. and Clegg, K. (2006). *Innovative assessment in higher education*. London: Routledge.

Juwah, C., Macfarlane-Dick, D., Matthew, B. Nicol, D., Ross, D. and Smith, B. (2004). *Enhancing student learning through effective formative feedback*. The Higher Education Academy: York, UK.

Krathwohl, D.R., Bloom, B.S., and Masia, B.B. (1969). *A taxonomy of educational objectives, the classification of educational goals, handbook II: affective domain*. New York: McKay.

LaSere Erickson, B. and Weltner Strommer, D. (1991). *Teaching College Freshman*. San Francisco: Jossey Bass.

Simpson, E.J. (1972). *The classification of educational objectives in the psychomotor domain*. Washington: Gryphon House.

Waugh, C.K. and Gronlund, N.E. (2012). *Assessment of student achievement. (10th ed.)* Pearson.

Five

Feedback as Practice in Dialogue

Student and Instructor Feedback

Giving feedback to students is an essential part of the learning process. Timely and appropriate feedback helps a student see what she or he has achieved in any given assignment and also shows where more work is needed in the future. It also serves to motivate students, as feedback shows not only that the instructor has read the assignment, but also that they have taken time to provide feedback on it. In other words, the feedback gives students a reason to write or create a presentation as they know their work will have a reader.

The type of feedback that is given depends on whether it is **formative** or **summative** feedback. Nevertheless, for any one program of study it is advisable to develop a template for feedback that all instructors use for different kinds of assignments. Some examples of templates are provided for summative feedback for a range of assessment types at different level of study are provided at the end of this section.

Formative feedback should be specific and highlight what a student did well, what he or she did not do so well and, very importantly, provide advice on how the student could have improved the assignment. The advice should be concrete and usable. It should address the student directly rather than in the third person.

For example, compare the following feedback:

- **Example 1**

> The bibliography and referencing are good. The student's argument is weak and is not convincing. It is difficult to see how the student's arguments relate to the essay question. She should work harder in future.

- **Example 2**

> **What is good:** Your framing of the issue is very good and you have made clear why a gender perspective is relevant in any investigation of the rising incidence of HIV in Japan. You also clearly define the scope of the essay and how you plan to address the issue, You have drawn on some excellent research, both secondary and primary, academic and popular, and used this to good effect in the essay.
> **What is not so good:** The essay could have been more tightly structured. You spent quite a lot of time going into background issues and therefore did not give sufficient attention to the specificities of the situation in Japan.
> **What you could do to improve:** You needed to relate all your arguments back to your main question, does a gender perspective help us understand the rise in the incidence of HIV in Japan. In a short essay it is often necessary to cut interesting data that is not directly relevant to your thesis statement. The introduction of some statistical data early on in the essay would also have helped the reader understand better the issue.

In example one, the student rather than a third person is addressed. The comments are vague and give no clear indication of why something is 'good' or 'bad'. In the second example, the student is addressed directly and clear reasons are given for the 'good', 'bad', and ways to 'improve' type comments.

Feedback on a written report should ideally include the following:

1) General comments about the assignment.
2) Specific comments (perhaps in text if the essay has been submitted electronically or in the margins if a hard copy submission.
3) Ideas for further reading.

Summative Feedback
Summative feedback is provided at the time that the assessment is carried out. Opinion is divided over whether detailed feedback is necessary or not. Some argue that at the end of a course it is sufficient simply to grade the essay. Personally we feel that providing the feedback is going to reach the student (i.e. the student is not leaving the area to return home) then it is helpful to give a final assessment of what the student has done well, what was not as good and what can be done to improve work in the future. The policy on summative feedback should be worked out by the program providers. The example given above for formative feedback could work just as well as summative feedback on an assignment.

Tone of Feedback
It is important that the feedback is encouraging, but does not give unrealistic ideas of competence or progress. At the same time, it is important to not be overly critical. The idea is to encourage and not 'put down' the student.

Things to Avoid:

- Being overly casual – as in 'you're getting quite good at this lark'.
- Being overly encouraging – 'This is incredible'.
- Being overly harsh, dismissive or sarcastic – 'You have not only failed to do x, y and z but on top of that you are poor at a, b, and c', or 'I wonder why you even bothered to hand this in…'
- Being overly intimate or chatty in the feedback. It's fine to make a brief personal comment, such as 'Thank you for your assignment. I know you have worked hard on this under quite difficult circumstances', but do not launch into your own personal stories about similar challenges you faced.[1]

Timeliness of Feedback
It is important that students get feedback on an assignment as soon as possible. A two week turn-around is the ideal time period between submission of work and receiving feedback. For some assignments it may be necessary to get back to the student more quickly than this. For example, if a student submits the text for a presentation that will be given the next day then clearly you have to give immediate feedback.

---

1) We are grateful to Alison Churchill, Director of Teaching and Learning Quality, Open College of the Arts, for her feedback and examples.

Instructor Feedback

It is now standard practice for students to be given the opportunity to evaluate a course instructor on her or his course at the end of a session. Feedback from such evaluations can provide important data about student perceptions and a degree of satisfaction. There are limits to this process, however, which will be outlined below.

We also find it useful to use a weekly comment sheet that enables instant feedback from students in an unstructured written form. This can also be used for taking attendance, although confidentially is then lost. Asking for specific feedback can also work well. For example, early on in a course, with a diverse student body, it is helpful to find out if they can follow your speed of speaking. A good reflective question that gives excellent feedback on a class is to ask students to write down the most important thing they learned in today's class.

Likewise, it is also interesting to ask students to write down one thing they felt needed more explanation. In our experience, students will often ask questions that have been raised by the class or request sources of further information on a topic in the comment sheet. These questions and requests can be followed up in the next class. When students realize that their voice is being heard they become more involved in the class and are more motivated to read and reflect on the reading materials that are given out.

When assessing final feedback, it is important to consider the following:

- Nature of the course – is this an elective or required subject. If a required subject, at what level? How large are the classes? Courses that are chosen rather than required, classes with less than 15 but more than 10 students, and 3rd and 4th year classes are generally rated higher than classes that are required, large, and at the lower levels.
- Who is taking this class? – Japanese students will generally rate low any questions that ask about their commitment or contribution to the class. They are less likely to rate low the instructor's efforts. If the class is reaching out to both specialist and general students, as is the case with the Osaka University Short-Term Student Exchange Program (OUSSEP) and classes that are also open to regular students in that faculty, there might be frustration that the level is not quite right. The level will be too low for the specialists and may be too difficult for the generalists.
- Do you need to talk with others who are teaching this group of students? It might be that students are giving similar feedback to all instructors, and, if so then there might be a need to overview the program.

Finally, when it comes to understanding feedback from students it can be very useful to do a pre-course questionnaire that asks about expectations for the class, experience with the proposed assessment methods (will extra support be needed), any special needs, including language support. This data not only helps in the delivery of the course, but also aids in the understanding of evaluative data collected at the end of the session.

Samples of Assessment Types with Instructions and Associated Feedback and Criteria

Here we provide some examples of assessment frameworks that make explicit reference to learning outcomes at both course and program level, in addition to examples of student feedback sheets, for courses in our Human Sciences International Undergraduate Degree Program.

Critical Thinking Skills (First Year Course)

**Critical Thinking Skills
(First Year Course)**

Assessment Tasks and Rationale
- Critical analysis of editorial (20%, due Week 8)
- Critical essay of 1,500 words (30%, due Week 15)
- Critical thinking portfolio (40%, due Week 15)
- Class participation (10%)

Critical Analysis of Editorial
For this assignment you are required to provide a brief (1,000 words) critical analysis of a newspaper editorial. The main aim of this assignment is to provide you with an opportunity to critically assess and critique a piece of text and demonstrate your awareness of common flaws and pitfalls in critical thinking.

The main focus will be on how you identify issues in critical thinking.

- Identify the main argument or claim that is being presented
- Provide analysis of the evidence the author uses to support their argument
- Identify any rhetorical devices, fallacies, or other issues you think are problems with the argument.

You can use either print or electronic editorials – make sure you provide a copy of the editorial with your critical analysis. We will consider this assignment in more detail during class sessions.

Critical Essay
For this assignment you are required to write a critical essay (1,500 words) on a topic of your choosing. The aim of the assignment is for you to practice constructing an argument that takes into account techniques and skills we have examined related to critical thinking.

The main focus will be on how you demonstrate critical thinking in practice.

You should aim to ensure that your essay:
- presents a clear argument
- has a clear and logical structure
- has a clear conclusion
- is appropriately referenced

While the topic of your essay alone is not particularly important, you should ensure that you select a topic that is of some interest to you, and possibly a reader, to have the best chance of constructing a good critical essay. Writing about something you have little or no interest in should *not* be an issue for this assignment! What I am interested in is your ability to construct an essay that shows some evidence of critical thinking. We will consider approaches to the essay in class sessions.

Class Participation
Attending scheduled classes and making an active effort to participate is important, as this will provide you with an opportunity to practice critical thinking skills (individually and in groups).

The main focus will be on how you engage with critical thinking issues and topics.

Critical Thinking Portfolio
In your portfolio you are required to collect examples of a range of arguments and fallacies. You need to collect 10 examples. In searching for examples, you can utilize books, magazines, newspapers, websites, or any other forum that you think might have some interesting examples. Your examples can include articles, advertisements, editorials, cartoons, blog entries, message board posts, letters to the editor, and so forth.

The main focus will be on how you identify and provide some analysis on common critical thinking problems in a range of different materials.

However, you are not to collect examples from textbooks on critical thinking or logic, and you can use each source only once for each example you wish to identify.

If you are utilizing a lengthy example (over 50 words) you should mark the section you are identifying for analysis. You should include enough of the source material to provide a reader with evidence to assess your claim. We will consider how to approach the portfolio during class sessions.

In your portfolio, each claim should be presented in the following format:

- Identify the fallacy/rhetorical device/strategy
- Provide a reference for the source
- Identify the issue in the form of a question
- Provide some brief analysis

Critical Thinking Skills
Assignment 1 Feedback – Analysis of Editorial

Critical Analysis of Editorial
For this assignment you were required to provide a brief (1,000 words) critical analysis of a newspaper editorial. The main aim of this assignment was to provide you with an opportunity to critically assess and critique a piece of text and demonstrate your awareness of common flaws and pitfalls in critical thinking.

The main focus is on how you identify issues in critical thinking.

- Identification of the main argument or claim that is being presented
- Some analysis of the evidence the author uses to support their argument
- Identification of any rhetorical devices, fallacies, or other issues you think are problems with the argument.

Identification of main argument	○ Clear identification of main argument and possibly identification of sub-arguments ○ Clear identification of main argument ○ Some attempt to identify main argument ○ No identification of main argument
Analysis of evidence used	○ Clear and detailed analysis of evidence used to support argument ○ Some analysis of evidence used to support argument ○ Some attempt at analysis ○ No clear analysis of evidence
Identification of rhetorical devices or fallacies	○ Clear identification and detailed analysis of devices and fallacies ○ Some identification and analysis of devices and fallacies ○ Some attempt at identification of devices and fallacies, but weak analysis ○ No clear identification of devices and fallacies
General (clarity of expression, grammar, presentation)	○ High standard of composition and expression ○ Acceptable level of composition and expression ○ Presentation weak in either clarity, grammar or presentation
General comments	
Mark	

Critical Thinking Skills
Assignment Feedback – Critical Essay

Critical Essay
For this assignment you were required to write a critical essay (of approximately 1,500 words) on a topic of your choosing. The aim of the assignment was for you to practice constructing an argument that takes into account techniques and skills we examined related to critical thinking.

The main focus is on how you demonstrate critical thinking in practice.

- Essay presents a clear argument
- Essay has a clear and logical structure
- Essay has a clear conclusion
- Essay is appropriately referenced

Main argument of essay	○ ○ ○ ○	Clear and persuasive argument and possibly sub-arguments Clear argument and sub-arguments Some attempt to present a main argument No main argument, or argument is very unclear or unconvincing
Clear and logical structure	○ ○ ○ ○	Clear and logical structure to support main argument Some structure provided Some attempt at providing structure, but unclear or unconvincing No clear evidence of supporting structure provided
Clear conclusion	○ ○ ○ ○	Clear and persuasive conclusion provided Clear conclusion provided, although not particularly persuasive Some attempt at providing a conclusion, but too brief or unclear No conclusion provided
General (clarity of expression, grammar, presentation)	○ ○ ○	High standard of composition and expression Acceptable level of composition and expression Weak in clarity, grammar or presentation
	Conclusion: *Reasons:* *Premises:*	
General comments		
Mark		

Critical Thinking Skills
Assignment Feedback – Critical Thinking Portfolio

In your portfolio you were required to collect examples of a range of arguments and fallacies. You needed to collect 10 examples. Examples could include articles, advertisements, editorials, cartoons, blog entries, message board posts, letters to the editor, and so forth.

The main focus is on how you identify and provide some analysis on common critical thinking problems in a range of different materials.

- Identification of the fallacy/rhetorical device/strategy in each example
- Identification of the main issue or argument that is presented in each example
- Some brief analysis of each example
- Reference for the sources

Identification of fallacy/rhetorical device/strategy	○ Clear and correct identification of fallacies ○ Clear identification of fallacies (not all will be correctly identified) ○ Some attempt to identify fallacies ○ No identification of fallacies or fallacies consistently incorrectly labelled
Identification of main issue or argument for each example	○ Clear and detailed identification of main issues in examples ○ Some identification of main issues in examples (possibly too brief) ○ Some attempt at identification of main issues (weak rationale given) ○ No clear identification of main issues
Analysis of examples	○ Clear and convincing analysis of fallacies/devices ○ Clear analysis of fallacies/devices ○ Some attempt at analysis of fallacies/devices ○ No clear analysis of fallacies/devices
Sources referenced	○ Clear and detailed references provided ○ Some references provided ○ No references provided
General (clarity of expression, grammar, presentation)	○ High standard of composition and expression ○ Acceptable level of composition and expression ○ Weak in clarity, grammar or presentation
General comments	
Mark	

Self, Identity and Society (First Year Course)

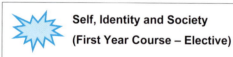
Self, Identity and Society
(First Year Course – Elective)

Overview

Assessment:
- Critical essay of 2,000 words (50%)
- Multimedia presentation (40%)
- Class participation (10%)

The course will be assessed by formative and summative assessment. Formative assessment will be undertaken throughout the term and consist of student participation in group practical activities and discussions. The summative assessment will comprise two tasks, performance on an individual critical essay on an agreed topic (50%) and performance on delivering a multimedia presentation (this can involve live presentation, a video presentation or involve a mix of different formats) to be delivered during the final two weeks of term (40%). The critical essay will require each student to prepare a 2,000 word scholarly essay on a topic that is developed in consultation with the instructor. The presentation will require students to deliver a critical presentation of no more than 10 minutes duration, in a format of their choice, on a topic or theme that is to be negotiated with the instructor. In addition, class participation will comprise 10% of the final course grade.

Critical Essay

2,000 Words
50% of final grade

For this essay you are required to provide a critical essay that considers a topic of clear relevance to general themes covered in the course. Your essay should focus on the interrelated concepts of self and identity and how these might be related to society.

Some possible areas of interest include:

- Comparison of different theories/conceptual approaches to self and identity
- Detailed review of a single theory/approach and how it relates to understandings of contemporary social issues
- "What if?" essay, that seeks to provide an account of what we might think about self and identity if particular historical/personal/conceptual things were changed (e.g., what would a modern psychology of identity look like if Freud's ideas had not been considered interesting or important)
- How a contemporary social issue, phenomenon or problem can be understood in light of a particular theory/theories of self and identity (e.g., gay and lesbian rights, ethnic and national identity politics, health and illness topics)
- Critique of contemporary understandings of self and identity
- Critique of disciplinary approaches to self and identity

You can also undertake an empirical essay project, which might involve utilizing source materials that you analyse. In other words, this would involve undertaking a small scale research project in which you:

- Describe and justify an approach to the exploration of self and identity
- Collect some data (e.g., magazine articles, advertisements, media reports, internet materials)
- Provide some analysis of the data that relates to your theoretical approach (e.g., you might examine some magazine advertisements of skin care products in Japan and provide an analysis of these in terms of a particular identity theory)

While I have specified a word requirement of 2,000 words, this is negotiable given the range of language skills and abilities of course participants.

Multimedia Presentation

Brief (see examples below)
40% of final grade

For the multimedia presentation you are required to produce a multimedia presentation that can involve live presentation, a video presentation or involve a mix of different formats. The topic can be related to your critical essay topic, or can be something completely different.

Some possible examples include:

- A brief (5 min) video presentation
- A brief (5 min) animation
- A presentation to the class (10 mins) that utilizes PowerPoint and other media
- A website (i.e., text based blog, video diary, wiki)
- A live "performance" (i.e., anything that would not be characterised as "bad street theatre"!)

You can do this in a group if you wish, however you need to ensure that each member's contribution is made clear to both me and the audience (i.e., your peers!).

I have included copies of the feedback sheets you will receive after the assignments have been marked and graded – this will give you a clear idea of what you will need to focus on when working on your essay and presentation.

Self, Identity and Society
Essay Criteria

	DESIRABLE FEATURES
Title	The title should reflect a) what kind of essay you are providing, and b) what your essay topic will be. For example: "A critical review of the utility of psychodynamic approaches to self and identity"; "An examination of how identity is constructed in online games"; "Race and ethnicity: Sociological approaches to self and identity"; "The evolution of self in contemporary thought"; "The social construction of terrorists"; "The presentation of 'natural femininity in Women's magazines: An analysis of hair care product advertising".
Abstract	The abstract should be clear, concise, and introduce the both the topic and what you intend to demonstrate with regards to the topic. Are you doing a critical review? A comparison between different theories/approaches? Examining empirical materials? Arguing that a particular idea or set of ideas is correct/incorrect? You should try to provide a *brief* overview or summary of your main argument.
Introduction	This should be clearly written and concise. The introduction should be brief and provide some comment on the topic and an overview of what you will be examining. A reader should get a clear sense of what your essay will be with regard to a) covering in terms of topics, and b) the general order in which you will be covering the topics.
MAIN BODY	
Well written	Your essay should be clearly structured and easy to understand. It should be written in an academic style with reference to relevant academic literature. Try to avoid the use of jargon or technical terms, particularly if you are unsure of their correct usage.
Topic	The topic of your essay should have clear relevance to the course materials. While you are free to choose the topic, you should ensure that you select a topic that will give you a good chance to demonstrate your ideas about "self, identity and society". You do not need to provide an exhaustive account – you just need to provide a sustained treatment of your chosen topic (e.g., you might focus on one particular aspect of a theory of self, compare several theories, apply a theory to some interesting examples, critique different approaches, provide a critical historical overview of a major figure or idea, and so forth).
Formatting	You should ensure your essay uses double-spacing, at least a 12 point sized font, and has your name at the top of each page. While you can use various formatting tools (e.g., bullet points, figures) try to keep these to a minimum.
Summary and conclusion	At the close of your essay, you should summarise your main points and provide a concluding statement. This should be consistent with your introduction.
REFERENCES	These should be complete and correctly formatted. Ensure you provide a single list of references presented alphabetically. There should be an exact match between the references cited in your analysis section and those that appear in your reference section. Harvard style should be utilized (for G30 students consult the "Writing and Style Guide").
Appendices	This is not required, but if you wish to provide additional materials (e.g., newspaper or magazine excerpts, photographs, transcripts of interviews) you can place these in an appendix at the end of your essay.
General	A poor essay will have deficiencies in all of the above. A good essay may have a number of problems in some areas, but there will be evidence of a considered attempt to produce a scholarly, academic essay that clearly has the theme of "self, identity and society" as its main concern. An excellent essay will generally adhere to the above in addition to providing a *convincing, interesting, possibly novel* account of a relevant topic to "self, identity and society".

Self, Identity and Society
Multimedia Presentation Criteria

	DESIRABLE FEATURES
Theme or topic	The topic or theme of your presentation should have clear relevance to the course materials. While you are free to choose the topic, you should ensure that you select a topic that will give you a good chance to demonstrate your ideas about "self, identity and society" in a multimedia format. You do not need to provide an exhaustive account – you just need to provide a brief, interesting and relevant presentation of your chosen topic (e.g., you might focus on one particular aspect of a theory of self, compare several theories, apply a theory to some interesting examples, critique different approaches, provide a critical historical overview of a major figure or idea, and so forth).
Practical issues	You should ensure your presentation can be given in a regular class session and is of a reasonable duration (i.e., no more than 10 mins). You may also want to consider providing opportunities for questions and feedback from your audience. Hand-outs or props can be quite useful to emphasize points or to stimulate discussion.
Format	Your presentation should have some form of introduction and a clear conclusion. Given the wide variety of presentation formats this is subject to a deal of subjectivity – however, you should ensure that the central theme, message or argument you are presenting is clear and related to the topic of self, identity and society.
Hand-outs	While hand-outs or other materials are not required, if you wish to provide additional materials (e.g., newspaper or magazine excerpts, photographs, transcripts of interviews) you should ensure these are relevant to your presentation, and that they are appropriately cited.
Content	You should try to ensure your presentation draws on relevant scholarly and academic sources. While it is perfectly acceptable to utilize a range of non-academic materials, you should take care to relate these back to themes on self and identity that are of a clearly scholarly nature. In short, you should try to make your presentation as interesting and as entertaining as possible – provided it can make some intellectual points!
General	A poor presentation will have deficiencies in all of the above. A good presentation may have a number of problems in some areas, but there will be evidence of a considered attempt to produce an interesting and relevant presentation that clearly has the theme of "self, identity and society" as its main concern. An excellent presentation will generally adhere to the above in addition to providing a convincing, interesting, possibly novel and entertaining account of a relevant topic to "self, identity and society"

Self, Identity and Society
Assignment 1 Feedback – Presentation

Presentation
For the multimedia presentation you were required to produce a multimedia presentation that could involve live presentation, a video presentation or involve a mix of different formats.

The main focus was on how you presented a critical account of a topic of relevance to conceptualizations of self and identity, and how these might be related to society.

Clear identification and description of the topic	○ Clear identification of the topic with detailed description ○ Clear identification of topic ○ Some attempt to identify topic but unclear ○ No clear identification of topic
Relevant and topical use of background material	○ Clear identification and detailed overview ○ Some identification and overview of relevant information ○ Some attempt at identification of relevant information, but weak or insufficient context ○ No clear identification of relevant background information
Evidence of relating broad topic to specific conceptualizations of self/identity	○ Clear and convincing links between topic and concepts relating to self/identity ○ Some limited connections between topic and concepts relating to self/identity ○ Some attempt at providing connections between topic and relevant concepts, but unconvincing ○ No clear links between topic and concepts relating to self/identity
Overall evaluation of critical issues	○ Comprehensive analysis of topic with some critical insights into self, identity and society ○ Some analysis of topic that makes connections with self, identity and society ○ Description of some relevant issues but lacking in detail or scope (e.g., insights unclear or unconvincing) ○ Insufficient or inconsistent information provided that does not identify relevant issues or connections
General (presentation format, multimedia use, use of slides or hand-outs, clarity of presentation, time management)	○ High standard of presentation with good use of audio-visual aids ○ Acceptable level of presentation ○ Presentation weak (e.g., poor time management, poor use of audio-visual aids, poor vocal delivery)
General comments	
Mark	

Cross-Cultural Psychology (Second Year Course)

Cross-Cultural Psychology
(Second Year Course – Elective)

ASSESSMENT

Assessment:
- Essay 2,000 words (50%)
- Online Journal (50%)

The course will be assessed by formative and summative assessment. Formative assessment will be undertaken throughout the term and consist of student participation in group practical activities and discussions. The summative assessment will comprise two tasks, performance on an individual essay (50%) and online journal (50%). The essay will require students to provide a critical essay that compares and contrasts different cultural understandings of a psychological phenomenon. The online journal (blog) requires students to create an online profile for an imaginary person (i.e., an avatar) from a culture different from their own, and to provide a regularly updated blog detailing the avatar's experiences in Japan. Students will also be required to comment on other student's blogs. These will be reviewed at the end of semester.

Cross-Cultural Psychology
Blog Assessment

Requirements
By the end of the semester you should have produced the following:

1 x Self Introduction
Here you just introduce yourself to your classmates and provide whatever background information you wish.

1 x Avatar Introduction
Here you introduce your avatar (person from a cultural background different from your own). You can do this in any way you feel is appropriate. You can include pictures, videos, music – anything that you think makes the avatar more realistic

3 x Comments on topics
Here you need to provide **3** posts that are related to topics/themes that we have covered in the course. You need to do these as your avatar. You do not need to provide lengthy posts, but they do need to somehow relate to a clear topic in cross-cultural psychology. As with the introduction, you are free to include any materials that you think are relevant or interesting. Including references or links to relevant research will be rewarded!

I have provided some sample questions/themes for these below.

2 + Comments on other people's posts
You should try and provide responses to other student's posts (at least 2). You can provide responses as yourself – in other words you do NOT have to pretend to be the avatar!

Sample Questions for Topics

(Note: I will provide an updated reference list for the readings given during class sessions. You can use these in your answers or as starting points for finding other information)

Topic: Development

- Describe how children are raised in your culture (i.e., choose a particular developmental stage).
- Do you think children in your culture are different or similar to children in other cultures?
- What has been the most significant stage in your development?

Topic: Language

- Describe something about how your culture uses words to express thoughts or beliefs in specific ways.
- Describe your experience of living in Japan in terms of your sense of time, place or space.
- Are there ways of speaking in your culture that are very different from other cultures?

Topic: Intelligence

- What kinds of things does your culture regard as intelligent (or not intelligent?).
- Does your culture have a kind of "cognitive style" that you see as very different from other cultures?
- Does your culture place much importance or emphasis on "intelligence"? Explain.

Topic: Emotion

- Does your culture have emotions (or emotion displays) that you think are very different from other cultures? Describe one by giving an example from your own experience.
- How do you deal with how people from different cultures express various emotions?
- What kinds of emotions are socially acceptable or not acceptable in your culture?

Topic: Personality

- Do you think your culture has particular personality types? Give some examples.
- How do people in your culture regard people from other cultures in terms of personality types?
- Are there any unique aspects to your culture in terms of personality?

Topic: Social Interaction

- Describe some common 'rules' for interacting with people in your culture.
- Have you experienced some 'cultural misunderstandings' with people from different cultures? Give some examples.
- What kinds of things do people from your culture do when interacting in public spaces?

Topic: Health and Well-Being

- What kinds of things are considered healthy or unhealthy in your culture?
- Does your culture have any psychological health issues that perhaps are not present in other cultures?
- What kinds of things do you think are very unhealthy or healthy in other cultures?

Cross-Cultural Psychology
Assignment Feedback – Critical Essay

Critical Essay
The essay required you to provide a critical essay that compares and contrasts different cultural understandings of a psychological phenomenon.

The main focus is on how you demonstrate a basic understanding of key themes and approaches in cross-cultural psychology.

In addition, your essay should:
- Provide a clear treatment of a psychological topic or theme from a cross-cultural perspective
- Draw upon appropriate scholarly literature related to cross-cultural psychology
- have a clear, logical structure (and ideally a clear argument/position)

Essay topic is clearly relevant to psychology	○ Provides an excellent analysis of a relevant psychological topic ○ Provides a good analysis of a relevant psychological topic ○ Some attempt to present analysis of a psychological topic, but lacking in detail ○ No appropriate analysis of a psychological topic
Attempts to apply a cross-cultural approach to relevant psychological topic	○ Convincing attempt to apply a cross-cultural approach to a relevant topic of inquiry ○ Clear and logical attempt to apply a cross-cultural approach to a relevant topic of inquiry ○ Some attempt at applying a cross-cultural approach to a relevant topic, but lacking in either detail, clarity or providing inconsistent arguments relating to the topic ○ No clear evidence of application of a cross-cultural approach to a relevant topic (i.e., essay fails to present a cross-cultural account)
Use of appropriate evidence	○ Excellent use of source materials (i.e., journal articles, research reports, scholarly sources) ○ Good use of source materials (i.e., psychology texts and books) ○ Some attempt at utilizing relevant source materials (e.g., relies too much on 1-2 textbooks and non-scholarly materials) ○ No appropriate use of source materials
General (clarity of expression, grammar, presentation)	○ High standard of composition and expression ○ Acceptable level of composition and expression ○ Weak in clarity, grammar or presentation
General comments	
Mark	

Cross-Cultural Psychology
Assignment Feedback – Blog

Blog
The blog assessment required you to participate on the "cross-cultural psychology" blog. You were required to provide (as a minimum) a self-introduction, an introduction from the perspective of your avatar (i.e., a person from a cultural background different from your own), three comments on topics and two comments on other students' messages.

The main focus is on how you demonstrate engagement with psychological ideas and issues from different cultural orientations.

Self-introduction	○	Provided clear self-introduction
	○	No introduction provided
Feedback		
Avatar introduction	○	Provided clear introduction
	○	No introduction provided
Feedback		
Topics	○	At least 3 new topics posted
	○	Fewer than 3 new topics posted
Feedback		
Comments on others	○	At least 2 comments posted on other students topics
	○	Fewer than 2 comments posted on other students topics
Feedback		
General comments		
Mark		

Qualitative Research Methods (Second Year Course)

Qualitative Research Methods
(Second Year Course - Core)

Assessment:
- Thematic analysis report (60%)
- Discourse analysis report (40%)

Assessment for the course comprises two research reports that require the analysis of qualitative data. The first report will require the use of thematic analysis (due mid-term) the second report will require the use of discourse analysis (due end of term).

For the thematic analysis assignment (60%) you are required to produce a report (approx. 2,000 words) that details a thematic analysis of data provided on the topic of 'friendship'. A complete data corpus (video, audio and transcriptions of five semi-structured interviews) will be provided and you will be required to undertake a thematic analysis of the data in a mini-report format. While you are required to report findings in a formal report format, the main focus of the assignment will be on the degree to which you can undertake a clearly thematic analysis of interview data.

For this discourse analysis assignment (40%) you will be provided with five data extracts (taken from the 'friendship' data corpus) and for each extract will be required to answer two questions relating to the identification and analysis of discursive devices and discourse features in the data (approx. 1,500 words). The main focus of the assignment will on the degree to which you can identify, describe and possibly analyse a range of discursive phenomenon present in interactional data.

Qualitative Research Methods
Assignment 1 Feedback – Thematic Analysis

Thematic Analysis
For the thematic analysis assignment you were to provide a complete (brief) report that details your attempt to provide a thematic analysis of selected 'friendship' data. While you were required to present your findings in a report format (with relevant sections) the main focus of my assessment of your work is on how you have provided a clearly thematic analysis of the data.

The main focus was on how you presented a thematic analysis of data related to the topic of 'friendship'.

Title, abstract, introduction	○ Clear identification of the topic, method of analysis, and main findings (i.e., main themes identified) ○ Identification of topic and method of analysis ○ Some attempt to identify topic and method but unclear ○ No clear identification of topic, method or findings
Relevant background material	○ Clear and detailed review of background literature relating to thematic analysis and topic of 'friendship' ○ Some identification and overview of relevant information ○ Some attempt at identification of relevant information, but weak or insufficient context ○ No clear identification of relevant background information
Analysis	○ Clear and convincing attempt to provide thematic analysis of the data, with good use of extracts and some summary findings (i.e., thematic map or overview of main themes provided) ○ Clear attempt to provide a thematic analysis, utilising extracts to support themes ○ Some attempt at providing thematic analysis, but unconvincing and lacking in detail (i.e., insufficient extracts or analytic comments that relate data to the topic of 'friendship') ○ No clear thematic analysis provided
Conclusion or summary of main findings	○ Comprehensive analysis provided of how themes identified relate to the topic of friendship, or detailed critical comments relating to strengths/weaknesses of thematic analysis ○ Some analysis of how themes identified relate to the topic of friendship ○ Description of some relevant issues regarding themes and topic of friendship but lacking in detail or scope (e.g., insights unclear or unconvincing) ○ Insufficient or inconsistent information provided that does not make clear link between themes and topic
General	○ High standard of presentation ○ Acceptable level of presentation ○ Presentation weak (e.g., numerous grammatical errors, missing information, poor presentation)
General comments	

5 Feedback as Practice in Dialogue

Qualitative Research Methods
Assignment 2 Feedback – Discourse Analysis

Discourse Analysis
For the discourse analysis assignment you were to provide answers to two questions for each of the five provided data extracts. In general terms, you were required to identify and describe what social actions were demonstrated in each extract and to provide some description (and possible analysis) of how such actions were produced and performed. Given the broad scope of the assignment you could draw upon a range of approaches to undertaking 'discourse analysis' which could include discursive psychology, conversation analysis, ethnomethodology, critical discourse analysis, or other approaches.

The main focus was on how you provided some identification, description and possibly analysis of a range of practices and devices in interactional data.

Question 1: What is getting 'done' in the extracts?	○ Clear identification and description (and possibly some insightful analysis) of at least one main action being performed ○ Identification and description of relevant action/s ○ Some attempt to identify and describe action/s but unclear ○ No clear identification or description of a relevant action
Question 2: What devices can be identified, and how do they function?	○ Clear and detailed identification and description (and possibly some insightful analysis) of at least one discursive device related to answer to Question 1 ○ Some identification and description of discursive device/s ○ Some attempt to identify and describe discursive device/s but unclear ○ No clear identification or description of any discursive device
Overall analysis	○ Clear and convincing attempt to provide discourse analysis to relevant data ○ Clear attempt to provide a discourse analysis ○ Some attempt at providing a discourse analysis but unconvincing and lacking in detail ○ No clear discourse analysis provided
Conclusion or summary of main findings (if present – note this is not required)	○ Comprehensive analysis provided of how discourse analysis relates to the topic of friendship, or detailed critical comments relating to strengths/weaknesses of discourse analysis ○ Some analysis of how data examined relates to the topic of friendship ○ Description of some relevant issues regarding discourse analysis and topic but lacking in detail or scope (e.g., insights unclear or unconvincing) ○ Insufficient or inconsistent information provided that does not make clear link between discourse analysis and topic
General	○ High standard of presentation ○ Acceptable level of presentation ○ Presentation weak (e.g., numerous grammatical errors, missing information, poor presentation)
General comments	

Introduction to Social Psychology (First Year Course)

Introduction to Social Psychology
(First Year Course – Elective)

Assessment:
- Examination (90%)
- Class participation (10%)

The examination (90 minutes) will require you to answer two essay questions from a choice of six. You will be provided with the questions well in advance of the exam, in addition to guidance on how to select an appropriate topic throughout the course. The main focus will be on how you synthesize a range of scholarly information to produce two critical essays that examine topics of contemporary relevance in social psychology.

In addition, class participation will comprise 10% of the final course grade.

FINAL EXAM: Introduction to Social Psychology (2012-13)
INSTRUCTIONS TO CANDIDATES

Answer **ONE** question from **Section A** and **ONE** question from **Section B**.

All questions carry equal marks. You are advised to spend approximately 45 minutes on each question.

Refer to evidence from the literature relevant to this course wherever appropriate in all your answers. You are permitted to bring one (1) page of notes into the examination.

SECTION A (50%)

1. Critically discuss the relationship between attitudes and behaviour in social psychology.

2. Critically discuss social psychological theories concerning attribution.

3. Critically discuss social psychological studies of conformity and/or obedience.

SECTION B (50%)

4. Critically discuss findings relating to how groups influence individual decision making.

5. Critically discuss social psychological theories of prejudice.

6. Describe and critically evaluate factors that social psychologists have identified that influence the likelihood of people engaging in prosocial behaviour.

Social Psychology Examination – Assessment Criteria

Essay 1

	Answer demonstrates (at least) a basic understanding of one or more key themes and approaches that relate to the topic
	Answer clearly utilizes evidence to present an argument
	Answer demonstrates some critical interpretation or evaluation of theories/research evidence related to the topic
	Answer provides accurate and relevant information drawn from social psychological sources
	Answer generally provides evidence of interpretation, evaluation and discussion of the topic with regard to social psychological themes and issues
	Answer is presented in a structured, essay format (rather than disconnected ideas or facts)
	Optional: Answer demonstrates an understanding of how theoretical perspectives from social psychology may inform our everyday understandings of the topic examined

General comments on essay:

Essay 2

	Answer demonstrates (at least) a basic understanding of one or more key themes and approaches that relate to the topic
	Answer clearly utilizes evidence to present an argument
	Answer demonstrates some critical interpretation or evaluation of theories/research evidence related to the topic
	Answer provides accurate and relevant information drawn from social psychological sources
	Answer generally provides evidence of interpretation, evaluation and discussion of the topic with regard to social psychological themes and issues
	Answer is presented in a structured, essay format (rather than disconnected ideas or facts)
	Optional: Answer demonstrates an understanding of how theoretical perspectives from social psychology may inform our everyday understandings of the topic examined

General comments on essay:

Peace and Conflict Studies I (Second Year Course)

Peace and Conflict Studies I
(Second Year Course – Core)

Assessment Tasks and Rationale
- Conflict mapping and assessment (2,000 – 3,000 words, 40%)
- Peace building presentation (40%)
- Reflective journal (20%)

Critical Essay
For this assignment you are required to produce a conflict map and assessment (2,000-3,000 words) that provides some critical analysis of a contemporary conflict. The focus of this report is to engage in a process of conflict assessment (utilizing a 'conflict mapping' approach if possible) that might assist in the development of possible solutions or strategies to deal with the main conflict issues. The broad aim of the assignment is for you to engage in a process of critical analysis of a real-world conflict that takes into account materials that we have examined related to peace and conflict analysis.

The main focus will be on how you demonstrate critical analysis of a contemporary conflict.

You should aim to ensure that your essay:
- presents a clear argument
- has a clear and logical structure
- has a clear conclusion
- is appropriately referenced

Presentation
The presentation assignment requires you to develop an approach to peace building (i.e., detailing positive solutions, outcomes or critical insights) towards the conflict previously examined in the critical essay, and give a presentation of your approach to the class of no more than 10 minutes duration.

The main focus will be on how you identify and communicate in presentation format an effective approach to peace building that relates to a real world conflict.

Reflective Journal
In your reflective journal you will be required to collect examples of contemporary media reports of conflict and peace related stories, with accompanying critical comments. You can utilize books, magazines, newspapers, websites, or any other forum that you think might have some interesting examples. Your examples can include articles, advertisements, editorials, cartoons, blog entries, message board posts, letters to the editor, and so forth.

Peace and Conflict Studies I
Assignment 1 Feedback – Conflict Mapping and Assessment

For this assignment you were required to write a report (no more than 3,000 words) which provides some critical analysis of a contemporary conflict. The focus of this report is to engage in a process of conflict assessment (utilizing a 'conflict mapping' approach if possible) that might assist in the development of possible solutions or strategies to deal with the main conflict issues.

The main focus is on how you demonstrate critical analysis of a contemporary conflict.

You should aim to ensure that your report:
- presents a clear description of the conflict examined
- provides some evidence of conflict assessment (i.e., identification of main conflict issues, background information, conflict parties and any other relevant factors)
- provides sufficient information on the conflict so that a reader can begin to develop an approach to resolving the conflict
- has a clear and logical structure
- is appropriately referenced (if required)

Clear identification and description of the conflict	○ Clear identification of the conflict with very detailed description ○ Clear identification of conflict ○ Some attempt to identify conflict but unclear description ○ No clear identification of conflict
Identification of conflict parties	○ Clear identification and detailed analysis of conflict parties ○ Some identification and analysis of conflict parties ○ Some attempt at identification of conflict parties, but weak or insufficient analysis ○ No clear identification of conflict parties
Analysis of background information relevant to the conflict	○ Clear and detailed analysis of background information that may be related to the conflict ○ Some analysis of relevant background information related to the conflict ○ Some attempt at providing relevant background materials ○ No clear identification or analysis of background information
Conflict assessment overall	○ Comprehensive analysis of conflict background, parties, issues and relevant factors ○ Some description of conflict background, parties, issues and relevant factors ○ Description of some relevant issues but lacking in detail or scope (e.g., information provided on only one or two areas) ○ Insufficient or inconsistent information provided that does not identify relevant conflict issues or assist with the development of potential conflict resolution strategies
General (clarity of expression, grammar, presentation)	○ High standard of composition and expression ○ Acceptable level of composition and expression ○ Presentation weak in either clarity, grammar or presentation
General comments	

Peace and Conflict Studies I
Assignment 2 Feedback – Peace Building Presentation

Presentation

The presentation assignment required you to develop an approach to peace building (i.e., detailing positive solutions, outcomes or critical insights) towards the conflict previously examined in the critical essay, and to give a presentation of your approach to the class of 5 to 10 minutes duration.

The main focus was on how you identified and communicated in a presentation format an effective approach to peace building that related to a real world conflict.

Clear identification and description of the conflict	○ Clear identification of the conflict with very detailed description ○ Clear identification of conflict ○ Some attempt to identify conflict but unclear description ○ No clear identification of conflict
Identification of conflict parties and background information relevant to the conflict	○ Clear identification and detailed analysis ○ Some identification and analysis of relevant information ○ Some attempt at identification of relevant information, but weak or insufficient analysis ○ No clear identification of conflict parties or relevant background information
Analysis of conflict with proposals for solutions or critical insights	○ Clear and detailed proposals or critical insights that are relevant to the conflict examined ○ Some limited proposals or insights that are relevant to the conflict examined ○ Some attempt at providing relevant proposals or insights ○ No clear proposals or insights provided relevant to the conflict
Overall quality of proposals or critical insights	○ Comprehensive analysis of conflict background, parties, issues with clear proposals or critical insights provided ○ Some description of conflict background, parties, issues with some proposals or critical insights provided ○ Description of some relevant issues but lacking in detail or scope (e.g., solutions or insights unclear or unconvincing) ○ Insufficient or inconsistent information provided that does not identify relevant conflict issues or assist with the development of potential conflict resolution strategies
General (presentation format, use of slides or hand-outs, clarity of presentation, time managements)	○ High standard of presentation with good use of audio-visual aids ○ Acceptable level of presentation ○ Presentation weak (e.g., poor time management, poor use of audio-visual aids, poor vocal delivery)
General comments	
Mark	

5 Feedback as Practice in Dialogue

Peace and Conflict Studies I
Assignment Feedback – Reflective Journal

Reflective Journal
In your reflective journal you were required to collect examples of contemporary media reports of conflict and peace related stories, with accompanying critical comments. You were permitted to utilize books, magazines, newspapers, websites or any other forum that you thought might have some interesting examples. Your examples could include articles, advertisements, editorials, cartoons, blog entries, message board posts, letters to the editor, and so forth.

Scope of materials collected	○ Excellent collection of materials with clear relevance to peace and conflict topics and themes ○ Good range of materials that generally have relevance to peace and conflict topics and themes ○ Some attempt to collect relevant materials that may be relevant to peace and conflict topics and themes ○ Poor attempt at providing relevant articles (i.e., insufficient materials, no clear relation to peace and conflict topics or themes)
Reflective comments	○ Evidence of consistent critical and insightful reflective commentary provided ○ Critical comments and reflections generally provided ○ Some attempt at providing reflective comments, but lacking in insight or focus (e.g., merely describing what was in original materials) ○ No clear evidence of critical commentary
General (clarity of expression, grammar, presentation)	○ High standard of composition and expression ○ Acceptable level of composition and expression ○ Weak in clarity, grammar or presentation
General comments	
Mark	

103

Six

Moderation
– Ensuring the Reliability and Validity of Assessment

Moderation refers to a variety of quality assurance processes and practices that are undertaken to ensure that assessments are carried out with consistency and fairness. In its most simple form, moderation might involve having work that has been graded by an examiner checked by another instructor. Moderation should not be approached as an afterthought to teaching and assessment, but be conceptualized as an important component of an overall teaching and learning strategy. It can be helpful to consider moderation practices at the initial stage of planning any assessment as this will extend through to initial and final grading.

Moderation can assist with the following issues:

- Is there consistency with marking criteria across assessments?
- Are course learning outcomes fairly and adequately assessed?
- Is variation in grades awarded reflective of clear differences in student attainment rather than inconsistencies in marking criteria (and criteria application)?
- Are academic standards being adhered to?
- Is student feedback appropriate?

Developing a robust moderation strategy involves considering both the pre-assessment phase (i.e., in initial assessment planning stages and prior to any formal assessment) and post-assessment phases (i.e., following marking and grading of formal assessments). In addition, moderation can occur before undertaking a complete marking of all student assessments (pre-moderation) by marking a sample of work (see Figure 6.1 for an overview of moderation phases).

Figure 6.1 *Moderation phases.*

As with the design and implementation, at whatever stage moderation is undertaken care should be directed towards ensuring that assessments are constructed and reviewed to ensure both validity of assessments and the reliability of assessments.

It is important to note that Japanese universities have generally not embraced a system of moderation, other than with the assessing of dissertations. As such, it may take much effort to convince colleagues of the efficacy or need for moderation. Nevertheless, given the importance of grading outcomes on students' lifestyles and careers, we would encourage all program providers to consider how some simple moderation mechanisms can be built in to the program.

One simple mechanism is grading workshops where instructors meet and look over a sample of assessment outcomes and discuss the reliability and validity of each. This obviously involved the building of trust, but this can only enhance the learning environment over the long term. In the following sections we give more substantive ideas about moderation, both internal and external, for those who want to fully embrace this best practice.

Internal Moderation

It can be useful to discuss draft assessments with colleagues to get feedback on areas which might prove to be difficult or problematic in obtaining an independent assessment. Courses with highly specialized content or unusual assessment forms may not be easily moderated and this should be taken into account in the planning stages. For example, making arrangements to video record presentations can provide a means by which moderation can take place. Ensuring that learning outcomes for a specific course are aligned with appropriate assessments is an important feature of any academic quality management program.

Opportunities for discussing assessment design enables problems and issues to be identified before any assessment items have been given to students. Moreover, having multiple perspectives and experiences to draw upon can certainly aide in ensuring greater alignment of standerds across instructors.

Peer moderation process should involve checking the following:

- Alignment of the assessment with the relevant learning outcomes.
- Clarity of the task description.
- Clarity of any additional rubric or guidance notes accompanying tasks.
- Criteria that are employed to mark the assessment.
- Available guidance for markers (e.g., model answers).
- Academic challenge of the tasks in relationship to the level.
- Workload/time requirements of the assessment tasks.

When assessments have been agreed, it is important that final assessment information be clearly communicated to students in order to support their learning and achievement.

Moderation of Assessment Marking and Results

Following the assessment event (i.e., when all work for a particular assessment has been submitted) it can be useful to undertake pre-moderation of a small sample of work. The aim here is not to generate extensive numerical data on reliability, but to provide an opportunity for assessors to engage in a 'trial run' with the use of criteria and descriptors. This involves one or more assessors examining a small sample of work and comparing assessment results and comments. This process can highlight possible issues with marking criteria and assessor application of criteria, and can provide valuable feedback on the fitness of purpose of particular elements of the assessment item.

Following pre-moderation, the full moderation of marking is generally undertaken by reviewing a sample of students' marked work rather than marking all student assessments. This involves the moderator reviewing (rather than marking in the full sense) an agreed sample of work to establish whether the marking is at the appropriate standard, consistent, and in line with the explicit assessment criteria.

Sampling of students' work should be representative both in terms of the sample size employed and the range of grade classifications examined. For example, with small numbers of students (i.e., 10-15 students) it might be appropriate to sample a larger range of work than with larger numbers of students (i.e., with 100 students it might be appropriate to sample 20%). It is important to include in any sample a range of grade classifications, and particular attention should be directed towards examining work that is close to a classification boundary (i.e., between an A and an S grade).

Moderation can also be completed in specific instances through double or team marking. In this case more than one marker independently marks student work. Double or team marking can be undertaken as **blind marking**, where each marker is unaware of the marks allocated by the other(s), or as second marking, where all markers are aware of the marks.

For full moderation, it is important that statistical analyses (i.e., computation of means and standard deviations) should be undertaken as part of the moderation process to identify anomalies and trends in final marking, which can then be addressed by further moderation practices.

Outcomes of Moderation Processes

In cases where differences remain unresolved in the moderation of marking it is important to have agreed procedures. This is to insure reliability of the assessment process and to assist in any potential dispute resolution (particularly when a student may challenge the mark, grade, or assessment process).

The marker and moderator should review the assessment criteria and their interpretation of them. If a divergence of understanding or interpretation is identified and resolved, re-marking and further moderation should be undertaken as appropriate.

If no divergence in interpretation of assessment criteria is identified but a difference in marking remains or if an identified divergence remains unresolved or if re-marking and further moderation still identify inconsistency between marker and moderator, the matter should be referred to someone external to this moderation. Outcomes might include:

- Arranging for an additional moderator to sample the student work.
- Arranging for an additional marker to mark all the students' work.
- Marking the assignment(s) her/himself.

It is important to consider that any external moderator or examiner should focus on assessing whether the standards achieved by students on a course or program are consistent with the specific learning outcomes and program level criteria, and that there is consistency and effectiveness in the assessment task.

Finally, it is important to ensure that documentary evidence is kept to enable review of the moderation processes, this will provide for a clear audit trail of the decision making process and can also be useful as feedback for the design and adjustment of other assessments.

External Moderation

External moderation involves having independent examiners review marked work, and is often employed with small samples of work drawn from a range of grade classifications. Here, the focus is often not on making alterations to marked work that is to be returned immediately to students, but on examining the robustness of marking and grading for a particular course over time. External moderation is most often used for large projects, thesis and dissertations, and can provide for valuable feedback provided external examiners are provided with clear information on the desired learning outcomes. One major disadvantage of external moderation is that it requires additional resources (e.g., time, additional personnel) and careful consideration should be given to maximizing the utility of any external moderation undertaking.

Course Leader Reports

An extremely useful practice that can assist with moderation (both internal and external) and course development involves the use of **course leader reports**. These reports aim to provide for a brief course evaluation after completion.

These reports can include a brief syllabus, details on learning outcomes and related assessment, student evaluations and some qualitative feedback on the course in general (e.g., problems that you may have encountered, recommendations for future course delivery). The idea is that someone who is not familiar with your course would be able to get a quick idea of what the course covered, how it was assessed, how students performed and what you had to say about how things went.

These reports are very useful for developing and extending quality assurance practices, course development, resourcing, staff development and a range of practical concerns (e.g., they are very useful for professors taking over previously taught courses). Importantly, they can also be used to bolster the credibility of an entire program when undertaken as a routine practice for all courses contained within a program.

We have included a course leader report example here that illustrates a number of the useful features that might be included in such reports. Note that, depending on the course you run, the format may be quite different from that in the sample report. The example we have provided includes information on the course aims and content, the course assessment, how the course assessment is linking (aligned) with the program level learning outcomes, summary of results for the course assessment, details on moderation, student feedback data and brief recommendations.

As you can see, the format of the sample report provides for sufficient coverage of the main issues we have focused on in this handbook, while still allowing a degree of flexibility to accommodate for a range of different course content and teaching styles.

Example of a Complete Course Leader Report

Course Leader Report

Course:	Critical Thinking Skills
Programme(s):	All-English Human Sciences
	All-English Chemistry/Biology Combined Major
	Core
Duration:	Half Year (Second Semester)
Code:	13A404
Academic Year:	2011 Second Semester
Course Leader	Dr Don Bysouth
Teaching Assistants	None
Report Date:	2012/03/06

1. Course Aims and Content

This course provided students with a range of tools and strategies for developing critical thinking skills that can be utilized in both university and everyday settings. The course drew on a range of disciplines to examine truth and knowledge claims by examining logic and reasoning, rhetoric and argumentation, perspective taking, propaganda, and the integration and synthesis of ideas. In addition, the course utilised ideas from enquiry based learning (EBL) to enable students to blend and generate ideas and empirical evidence from many different domains to enable an integrated approach to evaluating, challenging, and generating claims. The course also considered the role of critical thinking in relation to moral and ethical issues. Students undertook a blend of individual and group based activities examining truth claims in scholarly and mainstream media materials. The course was interdisciplinary in scope and drew upon a range of disciplines including education, psychology, and philosophy, and materials drawn from both academic and everyday settings.

The principle aims of the course were:
- To equip students with a range of thinking and learning strategies that foster critical thinking;
- To enable students to analyse, evaluate, and generate claims;
- To enable students to reflect and challenge their own thinking practices;

- To enable students to appreciate the value of critical thinking skills in both academic and everyday settings.

The key course learning outcomes were that students could (upon successful course completion):
- Identify, evaluate, and construct different forms of argument and persuasion;
- Identify rhetorical devices and strategies utilized in making truth claims;
- Recognize common fallacies in everyday reasoning;
- Use a range of resources, including primary research papers and information technology;
- Use evidence to support or challenge an argument;
- Demonstrate a range of transferable skills including oral and written communication, effective planning and organisation, and independence.

Course Content

	Topic
Week 1	**Introduction** What is critical thinking?
Week 2	**Identifying arguments** Consideration of how to identify an argument or claim
Week 3	**Descriptions and explanations** Focus on how descriptions are constructed in producing claims
Week 4	**Clarity and credibility** Examination of how to assess the clarity of an argument
Week 5	**Rhetorical devices and logical fallacies I** Examination of various rhetorical techniques and fallacies
Week 6	**Rhetorical devices and logical fallacies II** Further examination of rhetorical techniques and fallacies
Week 7	**Rhetorical devices and logical fallacies III** Examination and analysis of "real world" rhetoric and logical fallacies
Week 8	**Evaluating evidence** Evaluating factual claims
Week 9	**Rival causes workshop** Exploring how to identify rival causes for claims involving cause-effect
Week 10	**Critical reading and writing skills** Examination of various techniques to aid in critical reading and writing
Week 11	**Critical research skills** Consideration of various techniques to aid in undertaking critical research
Week 12	**Case Study – MMR, measles and autism** Students presented with an interrupted case study
Week 13	**Moral and ethical reasoning** Consideration of moral/ethical approaches to critical thinking

Week 14	**Case Study in Ethics – Drug sales and scientific research**
	Students presented with case study featuring ethical dilemmas
Week 15	**Revision/Review**
	Review of course topics and materials

The course was delivered with a mix of interactive lectures, group based activities, individual tasks and case studies.

Assessment Tasks and Rationale
- Critical analysis of editorial (20%, due Week 9)
- Critical essay of 1,500 words (30%, due Week 15)
- Critical thinking portfolio (40%, due Week 15)
- Class participation (10%)

Critical Analysis of Editorial (20%)
For this assignment students were required to provide a brief (1,000 words maximum) critical analysis of a newspaper editorial. The main aim of this assignment was to provide students with an opportunity to critically assess and critique a piece of text and demonstrate awareness of common flaws and pitfalls in critical thinking.

Critical Essay (30%)
For this assignment students were required to write a critical essay (1,500 words) on a topic of their choosing. The aim of the assignment was for students to practice constructing an argument that takes into account techniques and skills examined over the course related to critical thinking.

Critical Thinking Portfolio (40%)
The portfolio required students to collect examples of a range of arguments and fallacies and provide analysis of them. Students needed to collect 10 examples, which could be drawn from books, magazines, newspapers, websites, or any other forum that students identified might have some interesting examples. Examples could include articles, advertisements, editorials, cartoons, blog entries, message board posts, letters to the editor, and so forth.

Class Participation (10%)
Students were awarded marks for attending scheduled classes and making an active effort to participate (in order that they had an opportunity to practice critical thinking skills individually and in groups).

Course and Programme Level Learning Outcomes
The following section indicates which learning outcomes for this course matched level appropriate programme learning outcomes. Learning outcomes that may relate to the overall programme learning outcomes (or to key graduate attributes) are identified with the code G (general/generic).

Knowledge and Understanding.

G	Describe a range of thinking and learning strategies that foster critical thinking
G	Appreciate the value of critical thinking skills in both academic and everyday settings
G	Distinguish between different forms of argument and persuasion
G	Reflect upon and challenge your own thinking practices

Skills, Qualities and Attributes.

SK1	Identify, analyse and evaluate factual claims in a range of domains
SK1	Identify rhetorical devices and strategies utilized in making truth claims
G	Recognize common fallacies in everyday reasoning
SK1 SK4	Use a range of resources, including primary research papers and information technology
SK1 SK5	Use evidence to support or challenge an argument
SK1 SK5 SK6	Demonstrate a range of transferable skills including oral and written communication, effective planning and organisation, and independence

These outcomes were assessed by the **Critical Analysis of Editorial** (20%), **Critical Essay** (30%) and **Portfolio** (40%):

Knowledge and Understanding.

Essay	Describe a range of thinking and learning strategies that foster critical thinking
Editorial Essay Portfolio	Appreciate the value of critical thinking skills in both academic and everyday settings
Editorial Portfolio	Distinguish between different forms of argument and persuasion
Essay Portfolio	Reflect upon and challenge your own thinking practices

Skills, Qualities and Attributes.

Editorial Essay Portfolio	Identify, analyse and evaluate factual claims in a range of domains
Editorial Essay Portfolio	Identify rhetorical devices and strategies utilized in making truth claims
Editorial Portfolio	Recognize common fallacies in everyday reasoning
Editorial Essay Portfolio	Use a range of resources, including primary research papers and information technology
Essay	Use evidence to support or challenge an argument
Editorial Essay Portfolio	Demonstrate a range of transferable skills including oral and written communication, effective planning and organisation, and independence

2. Summary of Results

Results for individual assessments and overall course grades are presented below (note that data has been rounded to nearest whole number). Due to the small number of enrolled students care should be taken when interpreting any descriptive statistics.

All submitted student work was screened with an online anti-plagiarism application (plagarism-detect.com) and no evidence of plagiarism was detected.

Assignment 1 (20%)

Editorial Analysis	
N	21
Mean	89
SD	6
Median	90
Mode	90
Min	80
Max	95

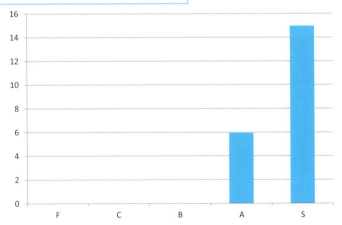

Figure 1: Distribution of Grades for Assignment 1 (Analysis of Editorial)

As can be seen in Figure 1 student performance on the editorial assessment was very high, with all students achieving high grades. What was particularly encouraging was the high number of students achieving an S grade, reflecting a very high standard of work.

Assignment 2 (30%)

Critical Essay	
N	21
Mean	86
SD	9
Median	85
Mode	85
Min	65
Max	95

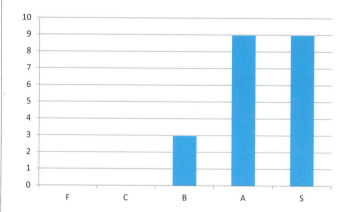

Figure 2: Distribution of Grades for Assignment 2 (Critical Essay)

As can be seen in Figure 2 student performance was lower on the essay task, however overall student work was of a consistently high quality.

Assignment 3 (40%)

Portfolio	
N	21
Mean	91
SD	5
Median	95
Mode	95
Min	80
Max	95

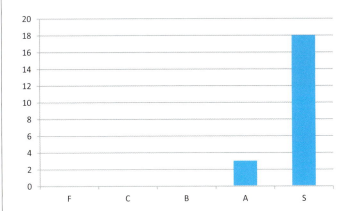

Figure 3: Distribution of Grades for Assignment 3 (Portfolio)

As can be seen in Figure 3 student performance on the portfolio was of a consistently high standard. What was very encouraging (as with the first assignment) was the high number of students achieving an S grade.

Final Grades

Final Grades	
N	21
Mean	90
SD	5
Median	91
Mode	96
Min	79
Max	96

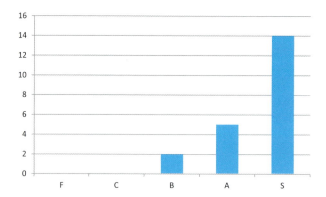

Figure 4: Distribution of Final Grades

As can be seen in Figure 4, students demonstrated high levels of achievement with regard to the course learning outcomes, and performance was significantly higher for the current student cohort in comparison to the previous semester cohort.

3. Moderation

Samples of the Critical Essay and Portfolio representing achievement at each grade band were examined at the G30 Moderation Workshop (23/02/2012). Feedback was that work examined adequately reflected the course marking criteria and learning outcomes.

4. Student Feedback

Student feedback was obtained via the use of a mid-term and end of term questionnaire (data presented below).

Mid-Term Student Evaluation Report
Critical Thinking – Don Bysouth
2011-2012
Registration = 24 (G30 JINKA Students = 9, CBCMP Students = 15)
Answer = 20

1. It is clear what I am expected to learn in this course

30%	60%		10%	
Strongly Agree	**Agree**	No Opinion	Disagree	Strongly Disagree

90% Strongly Agree or Agree

2. Class activities are helpful for my learning of the course material

45%	55%			
Strongly Agree	**Agree**	No Opinion	Disagree	Strongly Disagree

100% Strongly Agree or Agree

3. The assessment tasks are appropriate for the course objectives and learning outcomes

40%	55%	5%		
Strongly Agree	**Agree**	No Opinion	Disagree	Strongly Disagree

95% Strongly Agree or Agree

4. The assessment tasks were explained clearly

35%	45%	5%	15%	
Strongly Agree	**Agree**	No Opinion	Disagree	Strongly Disagree

80% Strongly Agree or Agree

5. I am satisfied with the level of support from the professor in this course

40%	50%	10%		
Strongly Agree	**Agree**	No Opinion	Disagree	Strongly Disagree

90% Strongly Agree or Agree

6. Overall I am satisfied with the quality of this course

35%	65%			
Strongly Agree	**Agree**	No Opinion	Disagree	Strongly Disagree

100% Strongly Agree or Agree

7. The professor communicates well with students

55% Strongly Agree	40% Agree	5% No Opinion	Disagree	Strongly Disagree

95% Strongly Agree or Agree

8. The professor demonstrates enthusiasm for the subject

60% Strongly Agree	35% Agree	No Opinion	5% Disagree	Strongly Disagree

95% Strongly Agree or Agree

9. It is clear what I am expected to learn in each weeks class

25% Strongly Agree	65% Agree	10% No Opinion	Disagree	Strongly Disagree

90% Strongly Agree or Agree

10. Classes are well organized

35% Strongly Agree	60% Agree	5% No Opinion	Disagree	Strongly Disagree

95% Strongly Agree or Agree

11. The professor explains the purpose of each class as it relates to the course

30% Strongly Agree	55% Agree	15% No Opinion	Disagree	Strongly Disagree

85% Strongly Agree or Agree

What are you enjoying most about the course?
Activities we do in a class is very helpful and fun. Also, visual aids help me understand the concepts of theory.
I enjoy the variety of examples that Don includes in his power point slides, because it helps me understand the concept better.
Very enlightening subject, taught well.
-Watching Videos   -Thinking critically
Looking at various techniques that many advertizments and articles, editorials are using in order to convince people.
Learning about every day fallacies in an academic manner. So much clear what's many with it.
The interaction between the professor & students.
The class power point presentations and the falt that the professor provides us with many examples relating to what we are learning. Having group activities.
That I get shown and practis new way of thinking and looking at things and fact.
I am satisfied with the course, and I enjoy what I am learning. The classes are interesting

and fun.
The enthusiasm in Don.
Pro. Don's "humor"<u>ous</u>
Don has a great sense of humor and for this abstract course, I feel that Don understands how far somethings there's no black and white such as what kind of evidence is usual to support.
Various interesting materials and examples presented by the professor.
Not heavy atmosphere.   Video clips.
Thinking like a philosopher.   Lots of interesting Videos.
Watch different kind of videos materials contains false / inprovince information and talk about it.
Instructor is humorous.
Professor is humorous.   Discussion after watching some video relate to the classes / lessons.
I like all of the examples in the power points.   A lot of them are from television shows or are commercials.   They are mostly interesting examples so they keep us engaged in the course.
Is there anything about the course you are not enjoying?
No
Nothing.
-Suffering from failed attempts at thinking.
I still find it difficult to determine what kind of fallacies / booby traps / rhetorical devices are used.
Maybe more student participation.
n/a
n/a
Nothing
Not really
I am enjoying it.
n/a
Some complex technical words, definition and meaning.   Cultural background is difficult to understand.
No.
Nothing.
No
Any other comments?
Professor Don is always very enthusiastic about what he is teaching.
Very good class, enjoyed by most of the students.
Some ideas are not general so that I cannot culturally understand it all.
No.
(   )
I wish he would be strict on time assignments students who hard in assignments late, they should be deducted points because it is not fair for other students.

No, not really.
No.
No.
No comment.
Nope! Thanks!
None
No.
Actually don't know how to write critical essay.
I actually don't know how to write critical essay.   I didn't learn it before so it was hard time to do assignment for me.
No.

2011 Autumn Semester Course Evaluation Report
Critical Thinking Skills – Don Bysouth
Registration = 24 (G30 JINKA Students = 9, CBCMP Students = 15)
Answer = 15

1. **It is clear what I am expected to learn in this course**

33%	60	7%		
Strongly Agree	**Agree**	No Opinion	Disagree	Strongly Disagree

93% Strongly Agree or Agree

2. **Class activities are helpful for my learning of the course material**

47%	53%			
Strongly Agree	**Agree**	No Opinion	Disagree	Strongly Disagree

100% Strongly Agree or Agree

3. **The assessment tasks are appropriate for the course objectives and learning outcomes**

20%	80%			
Strongly Agree	**Agree**	No Opinion	Disagree	Strongly Disagree

100% Strongly Agree or Agree

4. **The assessment tasks were explained clearly**

47%	53%			
Strongly Agree	**Agree**	No Opinion	Disagree	Strongly Disagree

100% Strongly Agree or Agree

5. **I am satisfied with the level of support from the professor in this course**

60%	40%			
Strongly Agree	Agree	No Opinion	Disagree	Strongly Disagree

100% Strongly Agree or Agree

6. Overall I am satisfied with the quality of this course

33%	67%			
Strongly Agree	**Agree**	No Opinion	Disagree	Strongly Disagree

100% Strongly Agree or Agree

7. The professor communicates well with students

53%	47%			
Strongly Agree	Agree	No Opinion	Disagree	Strongly Disagree

100% Strongly Agree or Agree

8. The professor demonstrates enthusiasm for the subject

73%	20%	7%		
Strongly Agree	Agree	No Opinion	Disagree	Strongly Disagree

93% Strongly Agree or Agree

9. It is clear what I am expected to learn in each weeks class

40%	60%			
Strongly Agree	**Agree**	No Opinion	Disagree	Strongly Disagree

100% Strongly Agree or Agree

10. Classes are well organized

40%	60%			
Strongly Agree	**Agree**	No Opinion	Disagree	Strongly Disagree

100% Strongly Agree or Agree

11. The professor explains the purpose of each class as it relates to the course

47%	53%			
Strongly Agree	**Agree**	No Opinion	Disagree	Strongly Disagree

100% Strongly Agree or Agree

What are you enjoying most about the course?
Different course materials every class; case studies helped me think critically even in real life.
When we are reading some articles, we discuss & analyzed the articles together.
jokes
Before this semester, I do not know anything about critical thinking. After this course finished, I can not say I master all knowledge but I get basic technics of critical thinking.
Learning how to have a clear structure to present an argument (in essays).
The use of real life examples and integrating them into class. The use of videos to gain students interest.

I liked all of the examples used in class; they were always interesting, but also relevant. I really enjoyed the last lecture too.   It really encouraged me to think.
I enjoyed this class!   Don is always enthusiastic.
The class is really interesting, and our activities are fun.
Clear explanations about controversial issues & new way of thinking.
Case study, Materials analysis.
Interesting way to look at things, learning useful skills.
The professor enthusiasm.
The contents.
Is there anything about the course you are not enjoying?
No
No
None
None.
None.
The course itself is more likely an elective, rather than a core course.
Occasionally Professor speaks a little bit fast.
No real complaints.
No
Any other comments?
Thank you for teaching this course.
None
None.
No. Thank you!
None.
Useful class.
No

5. Recommendations

Overall results and student feedback were highly encouraging and suggest the course is working well for both Human Science and Combined Major undergraduates.

As indicated in the last Critical Thinking Skills course leader report, some attention was directed towards ensuring that students with lower levels of English language skills were given additional appropriate support during the course. While the general standard of English appeared to be significantly higher with this student cohort, overall performance on assessment tasks and class interaction appeared to be generally of a much higher standard.

Professor	Date of Report
Don Bysouth	2012/03/06

Part Two

Reflections on Teaching and Learning on an English-medium Program

Guest contributions by

Viktoriya Kim
Saori Yasumoto
Christie Lam
Yukiko Ishikura

Seven

Introduction
– Teaching Reflections

Viktoriya Kim, Saori Yasumoto and Christie Lam

The rise of globalization in recent decades has led to an increasing emphasis on the need for higher education providers to engage in processes and practices of internationalization. In many societies, for example the USA, Australia, and countries in Europe (in addition Japan as a relative newcomer) student populations are increasingly multicultural due to greater migration flows. In such societies the development of internationalization of higher education policies often explicitly incorporates the notion that higher education must attend to the multicultural contexts in which teaching and learning occur. As a consequence, the multicultural classroom, which is characterized by a diversity of ethnicity, faith, first language and cultural traditions (e.g., Ben-Peretz et al., 2006), has perhaps become to represent the "standard" classroom (Tartwiji et al, 2008).

The emergence of the multicultural classroom has provided additional challenges for teaching and learning. What can educators do in terms of improving syllabus design? How can classroom discussion be effective when students have different levels of English and originate from varied cultural backgrounds? How can educators assess students' performance in a fair way when they have different learning styles and academic skills? How can the instructors and teaching assistants (TAs) give more efficient assistance in English-medium courses and multicultural classes?

In this chapter, our team, educators who have considerable experience of teaching and learning in the U.S., Australian and Japanese higher education systems, will share some teaching challenges we have faced in multicultural classrooms and provide suggestions that might assist instructors working in similar settings. Dr. Christie Lam completed her higher education in Hong Kong and Australia. Following the completion of her doctoral degree, she has taught in universities in Australia, Hong Kong and is currently working in Japan. Dr. Saori Yasumoto completed her doctoral degree in the U.S., and she has extensive teaching experience in the U.S. and Japan. Dr. Viktoriya Kim undertook her university education firstly in her home country of Kazakhstan and later pursued graduate studies in Japan.

Importantly, our experience of having been international students and now working as educators of students from diverse cultural and linguistic backgrounds enables us to deeply understand the importance of recognizing students' cultural differences. Indeed, such cultural differences may present significant implications for teaching and learning at the university level. Additionally, our team has a doctoral student, Yukiko Ishikura, who has been working as a senior teaching assistant (STA) since 2012 at Osaka University in Japan. Her rich experience in assisting students provides additional insights into the particular challenges facing TAs in English-medium courses in enhancing student learning.

Before we discuss the common teaching issues relating to the multicultural classroom, we would like to first give readers a brief background of the current trends of Japanese higher education system and how these relate to the increasing need to consider the importance of recognizing the need for cultural diversity awareness in the development and implementation of high quality degree programs. The multicultural classroom as a routine feature of the Japanese higher education sector, particularly within national universities, is a relatively recent development. This newer trend has been led by the increasing demand to create English-medium courses and programs in Japan. According to MEXT (2008), 194 universities at undergraduate level and 177 at graduate level offered English-medium courses as of 2007. The recent internationalization of university project Global 30 has further accelerated this trend. As part of this project, 33 undergraduate and 123 graduate English medium degree-seeking programs were newly created since 2009 (MEXT, 2014). Some of these degree programs have provided predominately English-medium courses offered to all students, while some have a more restricted scope and limit course offerings to international students only. Regardless of approach however, one of the more significant changes for Japanese higher education institutions is that classes have become considerably more multicultural in terms of students and instructors.

As a case in point, our team has developed and implemented courses for the Human Sciences International Undergraduate Degree Program at Osaka University, a four year undergraduate degree program. Osaka University launched the Human Sciences International program in 2011 (originally named as the G30 Human Sciences All-English Undergraduate Degree Program in keeping with the governments G30 promotion and branding strategy), and since then the International Program has recruited students from different countries. The course-offerings from this program has also attracted domestic students who seek to improve their English skills. While taking International Program classes, students are also able to gain opportunities to learn in a diverse cultural environment. Briefly, enrolments in individual courses are comprised of three different groups of students: (1) our program students (L1 English users or those with close to L1 English abilities), (2) Japanese students on mainstream programs and (3) Exchange Students (mostly from European countries, North American countries or other Asian countries). Such mixed classroom settings have generated additional new challenges in developing and implementing effective teaching and learning strategies. Our teaching experience has clearly shown that without cultural sensitivity to students' diverse backgrounds, we may undermine the students' motivation to learn.

In this chapter, drawing upon our team's critical reflections on our own teaching experience in the International Program, we would like to share some practical issues and solutions regarding teaching English-medium courses in multicultural classroom settings. The discussion is based on four main themes: **Syllabus Design**, **Assessment Approach**, **Classroom Management** and the **Roles of Teaching Assistants**. Bearing in mind that the major purpose of this chapter is not to provide universal solutions for teaching strategies in multicultural classrooms, but instead to raise relevant issues that may broaden an instructor's awareness of the dynamics of classroom settings and how these may impact on teaching and learning outcomes. We argue that it is critically important that instructors develop and facilitate learning environments in which students can benefit greatly from participating in *explicitly* multicultural settings. Therefore, we believe it is crucial that educators equip themselves with knowledge and skills so that they can work effectively with culturally diverse student populations, in addition to developing effective strategies to create classroom climates that affirm cultural diversity.

References

Ben-Peretz et al., (2006). Classroom management in multicultural classrooms in an immigrant country: The case of Israel. In C. M. Evertson and C. S. Weinstein (Eds.), *Handbook of classroom management: Research, practice, and contemporary Issues.* London: Lawrence Erlbaum Associates.

MEXT. (2008). *White Paper on Education, Culture, Sports, Science and Technology.* [http://www.mext.go.jp/b_menu/hakusho/html/hpab200801/1292564.htm]

MEXT. (2014). *Global 30: Present and future.* Paper presented at the Global 30 Symposium.

Tartwiji, J. V. et al., (2008). Teachers' practical knowledge about classroom management in multicultural classrooms. *Teaching and Teacher Education, 25*(3), 453-460.

Eight

Syllabus Design

Viktoriya Kim

In this section, I will introduce approaches to syllabus design by examining how to integrate syllabi into a wider curriculum (curriculum alignment by concept mapping), provide some practical advice for syllabus design, and consider some important points and issues when designing syllabi for a multicultural student body. Much of this advice is based on feedback I have received over several years teaching from students, in addition to professional development activities including faculty development workshops and moderation meetings.

Just as each course taught in our Human Sciences International Program is part of the curriculum of the program, each syllabus is an important piece of information about the whole. It is important to explain to students what they are supposed to learn from a particular course (purposes and contents), how the instructor connects course content with specific outcomes (assignments and assessment), how the course will deepen and broaden their knowledge (outcomes they aim to achieve), as well as what are the rules of the course. In this regard, it is important to note that an effective syllabus may serve a number of interrelated purposes, such as "setting tone of the course, a type of motivation for students to reach their academic goals, a planning tool for faculty, structuring tool of the students' work, and a contract between faculty and students about the expectations" (e.g., Matejka and Kurke, 1994; Tokatli and Kesli, 2009).

Therefore, when designing contents, assessment and outcomes of the course, I, particularly, pay attention to:
- Integrate the course into the curriculum and align learning outcomes of the course with those stipulated for this particular year of study;

- Communicate the structure and goals of the course with students; And
- Explain the rules of the course.

To achieve these purposes, I use the idea of *concept mapping*:

> A concept map is a two-dimensional, hierarchical node-link diagram that depicts the structure of knowledge within a scientific discipline as viewed by a student, an instructor or an expert in a field or subfield. (...) Faculty have used concept maps to organize their ideas in preparation for instruction, as a graphic organizer during class, and as a way to encourage students to reflect on their own knowledge and to work together and share their understandings in collaborative group settings.[1]

Curriculum alignment by the concept mapping of courses allows us to position the course within the curriculum and set its relative position with courses that have been already taught, courses that are being taught in parallel, and courses that will be taught later. In addition, this facilitates the delivery of specified learning outcomes and specific content of the course to students.

Syllabus Design through Concept Mapping: Integration of the Course into the Curriculum

There are two main ways to integrate a course into the curriculum: *vertical* and *horizontal* integration. Vertical integration allows for deepening knowledge on the subject based on previous introductory courses in the field, while horizontal integration is related to broadening one's knowledge in that particular field.

Let us examine how one of my courses that is taught in the 5th semester, Ethnographic Fieldwork, can be aligned vertically and horizontally with other courses in the program. As shown on the map below (Figure 1), Ethnographic Fieldwork can be considered as a continuation of the introductory course on Anthropology I and the more advanced course, Anthropology II. Therefore, when designing the course content of the Ethnographic Fieldwork course, it was necessary to consider what students have already studied and which topics need further development.[2] By the time they take a course on ethnographic

---

1) Zeilik, M. (n.d.). *Concept Mapping*. (http://www.flaguide.org/extra/download/cat/conmap/conmap.pdf).

2) In this case, students who have taken the Anthropology I course are expected to know what is anthropology, what key theoretical perspectives as well as what is the meaning of culture, and they should already be familiar with the main method of anthropological enquiry – fieldwork. In the Anthropology II course, they would have

fieldwork, students are expected to know about a range of methods and topics drawn from an anthropological approach, but require a deeper understanding of how these might be utilized to do ethnography. This then is what I will teach them in my course: where to start, how to prepare, what is needed to conduct a fieldwork and so on (Figure 8.1, Table 8.1).

Thus, *vertical integration of the course allows navigating which skills students possess and which ones need further development*, as well as what

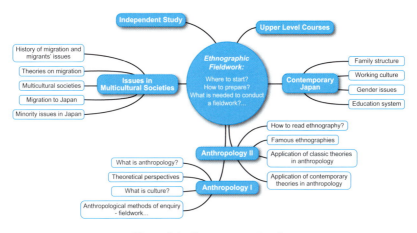

Figure 8.1 *Concept mapping 1.*

Week	Topic	Class Activity	Readings
1.	**Introduction to Course**. What is Ethnographic Fieldwork?		
2.	**Part 1: Ethnographic Research Methods and Issues.** Approaches to Ethnography and Fieldwork		
3.	Choosing a Fieldwork Site and Gaining Entry	Planning individual fieldwork	Reading 1
4.	In and About the Ethnographic Field: Participating, Observing, and Making Notes.	Writing a request letter	Reading 2
5.	Ethnographic Interviews.	Writing a set of interview questions	Reading 3

Table 8.1 *Ethnographic fieldwork syllabus*

deepened their knowledge further through reading famous ethnographies and learning about the application of classic theories and contemporary theories to anthropology.

skills they might need for subjects that will be taught in the following semesters.

With regard to ensuring horizontal integration, it is important to relate our Ethnographic Fieldwork course with a range of other topic-based courses that provide general knowledge about society, education, and social issues (e.g., Contemporary Japan, Gender Studies, Social Stratification in Japan, Issues in Multicultural Societies). Some of these courses focus on different areas and countries, while others focus particularly on Japan. Since basic courses on anthropology focus on the most famous ethnographies, for my course I choose mostly ethnographies that focus on Japan.

There are two main purposes of doing this focus on Japan: to deepen and broaden knowledge about Japan and its culture, and, second, to analyse how ethnographies discuss and interpret Japanese culture. Since there are students with various needs and interests, in the first classes I offer students a list of works that have utilized ethnographic fieldwork in Japan. Students and I choose the reading assignment together from the list. By doing so, students are encouraged in critically reading materials and getting clues that might be of use for their own projects.

I consider this part of syllabus design as one of the most important steps, since it guides the course design by providing general ideas on the topics and/ or methods that should be covered. In short, the end result is likely to be a more helpful course for students who take it. However, I must mention that the process of integrating courses is difficult to accomplish without student feedback, effective communication between faculty members, and participation in moderation workshops.

Course Content and Students' Learning Process: Positioning the Course and Setting Goals

Students usually have different goals, ways of understanding and learning course content, and divergent expectations towards the topics discussed throughout the course. Therefore, I also use the idea of concept mapping to ensure that the goal of each course is easy to comprehend. The use of concept maps for the development and teaching of course content is beneficial not only for students, but also for instructors, since they help to clarify gaps and deficits at the earlier stages of course delivery.

There are two main ways to using concept maps: one shows the instructor's vision of the connection between contents of the course, while another asks students to come up with their own vision of the connection between topics taught in the course and how they can be related to the discipline overall.

8 Syllabus Design

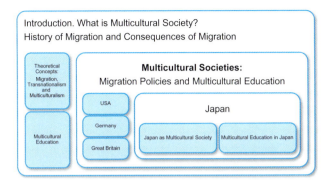

Figure 8.2 *Concept mapping 2.*

In the case of an instructor's concept map, *it is important to return to the map at the beginning of each lecture to identify what has been done and what topics are ahead, so it is clear for students at what stage of the course they are at any particular moment.*

Above is an example from the course on multicultural societies, which I have been modifying in the process of course delivery and reflecting on the students' feedback (Figure 8.2). This concept map helps students to generate ideas on how the course is delivered, what theoretical concepts will be discussed, and which countries they will study. Also, it provides information on the proportion of classes that will be devoted to each topic, how each individual class session is related to each other and so forth.

Another way for students to make sense of the course content is to encourage them to construct their own map. Making a concept map will be their first activity during the first lecture. After explaining the content, assignments, learning outcomes, and other details of the course to students, I then ask students to discuss in groups how they understand the connection between the topics and to produce a map based on their vision.

The following figure (Figure 8.3) illustrates some examples that first year students (enrolled in 2014) came up with at the beginning of the Introduction to Sociology course. In case of the students' concept maps, it is also important to reflect on students' understanding of content at the final stages of the course, reflect on how their ideas have changed, and discuss if they would like to edit the structure of the map, what they thought was lacking, what was unnecessary and so on.

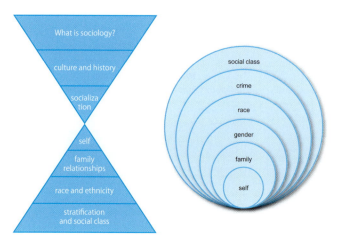

Figure 8.3 *Students' concept maps.*

Syllabus as a 'Learning Contract': Communicating Rules and Conditions of the Course

The discussion of the aforementioned topics assumes an active role of the instructor (professor) and students in constructing the syllabus, and in this sense both the syllabus content and structure of the course are open to negotiation. However, as was mentioned earlier in the book, *the syllabus is also a 'learning contract' between professor and students.* By clearly stating course content, specifying learning outcomes, and providing clear information on how the course will be delivered an instructor makes clear what kind of services they will provide.

The 'contract' must also include a clear picture of the types of assignments to be undertaken and requests to students, so they can know beforehand what kind of tasks they need to accomplish, how they can get better grades and how they will be evaluated.

In addition, *the idea of syllabus as a 'learning contract' becomes extremely important when teaching students from various cultures and educational systems, since it helps dealing with a wide range of students' understandings, expectations and attitude towards the course, its rules and conditions.* It eliminates many misunderstandings related to class proceedings and conduct, and by registering for this course students agree to subscribe to this "contract".

Table 8.2 is an example based on general rules decided by our International Program teaching team regarding our courses.

Assessment Requirements	Attendance at 80% of all sessions is required. If you cannot attend scheduled sessions due to illness, make sure to provide medical certificate; in case of unavoidable circumstances, please ensure that you notify your instructor via email or phone. Failure to attend three or more scheduled classes may result in being awarded a failing grade for the entire course. In addition, late attendance for scheduled classes may result in penalties.
	If you are unable (or have been unable) to conduct a presentation, or to sit all or part of an examination due to illness or other unavoidable circumstances, you must submit a notification of absence from a class promptly. If your absence is due to illness, please append a medical certificate. In other cases, please append a written explanation with an appropriate certificate. A supplementary time for presentation/examination may be arranged if deemed appropriate by the instructor.
	With regard to the method, location and deadline for the submission of essays/reports, please follow the instructions of the instructor. Once the submission period and the acceptance period have passed, no assignments can be accepted, whatever the reason for the delay.
	If you are enrolled in the course you are expected to submit all required assessment items, have met the minimum course attendance requirements, and completed all other work as directed by the course instructor. Failure to do so may result in you receiving a failing grade for the entire course.
	Academic misconduct (cheating, collusion, plagiarism or falsification of information) in all forms of written work, presentations, in-class tests and examination can lead to consequences ranging from loss of marks in the relevant course to zero grades for all classes taken that semester.

Table 8.2 *Course rules and conditions.*

Conclusion: Syllabus as a Tool for Better Learning

In this section, I provided an account of how the syllabus can be an important tool for instructors and students alike, drawing from my own experiences on developing and implementing undergraduate level degree courses. The syllabus can be an effective tool for having a more integrated and clear learning process, assist in communicating the structure and goals of the course, and promote the establishment of a 'contract' between students and professors regarding course methods and rules. I also provided a brief illustration of how concept mapping can be used to design more effective course syllabi.

The vertical and horizontal integration of a specific course into a wider curriculum by means of a syllabus allows students to understand what knowledge or skills they already possess or are expected to possess, what knowledge or skills they will acquire in the course, and allows professors to better plan their classes based on what their students have already studied and what skills need further development. The syllabus also sets goals for students to achieve and for professors to deliver and assess; these goals may present the instructor's vision or may be constructed by the instructor together with the students. In any case, it is important that in the lecture it is made clear for students and professors at what stage of the course they are towards achieving set goals, showing what has been done and what is ahead. Finally, I argued that the syllabus can be seen as a 'learning contract' between professor and students, making sure that professors and students are at an understanding regarding what are the course's contents, learning outcomes class proceedings, required assignments, evaluation methods, and class rules.

References
Matejka, K., and Kurke, L. B. (1994). Designing a Great Syllabus. *College Teaching*, *42*(3), 115-117.
Tokatli, A. M., and Kesli, Y. (2009). *Syllabus: How Much Does It Contribute to the Effective Communication with the Students?* Paper presented at the World Conference on Educational Sciences, 2009.
Zeilik, M. (n.d.). *Concept Mapping.* (http://www.flaguide.org/extra/download/cat/conmap/conmap.pdf).

Nine

Assessment Issues in Multicultural Classrooms

Saori Yasumoto

In this section, I will talk about issues related to the process of assessment by using my personal experience as an example. Because the way to evaluate students' achievement is related to our teaching philosophy, there are multiple assessment approaches. Therefore, I would like to emphasize that the following is just an example. Yet, I hope this section will provide an opportunity for readers to think once again about assessment process.

What are the Goals of Assessment?

Grading and assessing students' achievement consistently, rigorously and fairly takes a tremendous amount of time and energy. I believe that almost all instructors would agree with me on this point. We still provide exams and assignments in order to give grades for students. Why do we do so? One significant reason is that we are expected to submit grades to our school system and fulfil institutional, administrative requirements. But I also believe that the primary purpose of assessment is to encourage students to move on to the next level in the learning process. By having this statement as the main goal, I try to approach the assessment as a mutual learning place between instructors and students. In addition, I pay great attention to 'fairness' to evaluate students.

Assessment as a Mutural Learning Place between Instructors and Students

Vygotsky (1978) famously argued that instructors can guide students to maximize their problem solving skills. More recently York (2003) has argued that

that 'the teacher/tester and student *collaborate* actively to produce a best performance' (p. 478). Because I agree with their approach, I try to explicitly adopt a role where I navigate students by paying attention to three points:

1) Distinguish Types of Knowledge
There are mainly two types of goals that I expect students to achieve throughout the semester: 1) being able to understand basic knowledge, and 2) being able to apply this basic knowledge. Comprehension of basic knowledge can be done through reading and memorization. I usually check basic knowledge of the subject toward the beginning of the semester (i.e., before the 5th week in a 15 week course) by providing an exam. Because the main purpose of this stage is to assess whether students have an understanding of the basic concepts, ideas and definitions of a particular topic, I emphasize asking straight forward 'descriptive' type questions rather than questions that require explicit critical and analytical skills. I also provide a study guide (i.e., a list of concepts, terms, and theories) a week before the exam date to clearly set my expectations.

Once students have acquired an understanding of the basic course specific knowledge, they will move onto the next stage which is the explicit application of basic knowledge. Students will learn to critically, analytically and creatively think by applying terms, concepts and definitions that they have learned. To develop students' application skills, I provide a multiple writing assignments (i.e., two short essays and one research paper). I communicate the goals and assessment criteria of each assignment in advance with students (i.e., the instructions for the writing assignment, the grading rubric).

I prefer to provide multiple writing assignments because I can then see the progress of students. They usually incorporate comments and suggestions that I provided from the previous assignment. In fact, students tend to do better every time they submit a writing assignment.

When students do well on an exam but exhibit mediocre performance on an essay assessment, two reasons can be considered. First, is that these students are simply good at memorization types of examinations rather than writing an essay. Second is that students have not fully understood the basic concepts, terms and definitions that go beyond memorization of words. When I detect the latter case, I encourage students to learn basic knowledge once again.

Technical Tips to Provide Comments and Suggestions
My hope is that students can develop knowledge and skills over the semester by doing a multiple assignments, I use feedback to communicate with students. Four quick tips that I use to enhance the students' learning are:

- **Return Feedback Within 7 Days (or by the Next Class)**
  As I stated earlier, I assign a series of assignments for a given course that are undertaken across the semester. Based on my comments and suggestions on the first assignment, students are encouraged to work on the second assignment. Therefore, providing some quick feedback is necessary. Also, it is important to consider that students may care more about an instructor's reaction than most instructors might assume. Students may think that we are careless about their work, and/or that assignments are meaningless if we delay providing feedback.

- **Provide Both Positive and Negative Points**
  When I return students' writing assignments, I mention both positive and negative aspects of their paper. The positive comments can relate to writing style and grammar (i.e., clearly written without making grammatical mistakes; use of appropriate citations) and/or ideas (i.e., critically pointed out the issues, nicely applied learned concepts). I usually write how they did well first, then provide comments on how they can improve their paper by pointing out what is missing.

- **Avoid a Red Colour for Marking**
  When I was a graduate student, one of my professors used a blue pen to give students feedback because he believed that comments and suggestions written in a red colour ink have a connotation to show instructors' power and authority. He said that comments and suggestions written in a red colour ink can intimidate students which discourage them from learning. Following his suggestion, I avoid using a red colour ink whether I hand write or type comments/suggestions (see Rutchick, Slepian and Ferris, 2010).

- **Extra Points Approach Works Better than Deducting Points Approach**
  Based on my experience, students often work harder when they are given an opportunity to earn extra points rather than losing points when their work is formally assessed – but also on matters of general academic conduct. For example, when I would like students to come to class on time, I add the sentence in the syllabus that 'students who come to class on time will get two extra points toward the first exam' instead of saying 'students who come to class late will lose points for tardiness.'

2) Understand the Students' Backgrounds

I believe that understanding students' backgrouds is important, especially when we assess diverse groups of students. For example, the acquisition of language level is directly related to students' writing ability. Some students may have excellent ideas, but they may have insufficiently developed skills to enable them to effectively describe complex ideas in particular language contexts and settings. If I know this is the case, I take the situation into consideration. I pay great attention to students thinking processes rather than their writing style and skills.

- **Assessment Based on the Principle of Fairness**

When I teach diverse groups of students, I try my best to 'fairly' evaluate students' achivement. As I mentioned in the previous section, the levels of language skills can vary among students. Some students may be good at taking an exam based on multiple-choice questions, but other students may prefer writing essays. Because I hope to assess students' achievements holistically, I try to mix up various forms of assessments.

To illustrate how I approach assessment, I will introduce an example from one of my classes (Table 9.1).

In this class, students are asked to complete seven assignments during the semester. Each assignment has a slightly different weighting toward the final grade: Exam (20%), Journal (10%), Report 1 (10%), Report 2 (10%), Report 3 (20%), Report 4 (10%) and Presentation (10%).

From giving an exam, I evaluate whether students have demonstrated understandings of basic course specific knowledge (i.e., concepts, terms and definitions). I also make sure to use various forms of questions in any given exam: multiple-choice questions, true-false questions, matching questions, short answer questions, and essay questions. By doing so, I hope that students with various backgrounds (i.e., students who are good at answering multiple-questions, students who are good at answering essay questions) can earn points from what they have studied for an exam.

I use an in-class journal assignment to check whether students read their reading assignment before coming to class. I can also utilize this to evaluate the ways in which students demonstrate their understandings of assigned reading assignments from responses provided in the in-class journal assignment. Because I use this assignment to encourage students to read, I give them a good mark if I can see students' effort even if students cannot fully answer the journal topics.

Reports 1, 2 and 4 comprise a series involving the same writing assignment (i.e., two to three pages long). For example, I may ask students to find three newspaper articles to analyse throughout the semester. Because I use

Exam	20%	The format of exam will be a combination of multiple-choice questions, short answer questions, and essay questions. (A study guide will be provided.)
Journal	10%	This is in-class activity. You will be asked to write 10 journal entries during the semester. The primary purpose of this activity is to help you to clarify your thoughts and identify questions and discoveries. For that reason, journal entries will be graded based on originality, clear expression of your ideas, and thoughtfulness, and demonstration of critical thinking. I only accept journals that are written in class.
Report 1	10%	The details will be announced in class.
Report 2	10%	The details will be announced in class.
Report 3	20%	The details will be announced in class.
Report 4	10%	The details will be announced in class.
Presentation	10%	The details will be announced in class.
Attendance	10%	100 points: Perfect attendance or missed class once 90 points: Missed two or three classes

Table 9.1 *Assessment example.*

writing assignments to evaluate whether students have acquired skills to apply basic knowledge (i.e., concepts, terms and definitions), I instruct students to incorporate knowledge from class materials. I hope to see the development of students' writing, therefore, I give a gap between each assignment's due dates. As I mentioned before, I return assignments with comments and suggestions within a week so that students have sufficient time to reflect on the provided feedback, and hopefully incorporate new insights or knowledge into the on-going work for their next assignments.

Report 3 and the presentation can be combined. For example, I may ask students to conduct a mini-survey or interview to write a paper (report 3). Then students are expected to present their findings. Again, I provide comments and suggestions for report 3 before the presentation assignment. In this way, students will have a chance again to think about the assignment before the due date.

References

Rutchick, A.M., Slepian, M.L. and Ferris, B.D. (2010). The pen is mightier than the word: Object priming of evaluative standards. *European Journal of Social Psychology, 40*(5), 704-708.

Vygotsky, L.S. (1978). *Mind in society: the development of higher psychological processes.* Cambridge, MA: Harvard University Press.

York, N. (2003). Formative assessment in higher education: Moves toward theory and the enhancement of pedagogic practice. *Higher Education, 45,* 477-501.

Ten

Management Issues in Multicultural Classrooms

Christie Lam

In this section, I will share my personal experiences concerning how I manage the challenges of multicultural classrooms by paying attention to relationships between instructor and students, as well as among students, course content and teaching styles. I hope this section can help readers to establish a more positive, friendly and active learning atmosphere in the classroom.

Challenges for Delivering Lectures in the Multicultural Classroom

Classroom management plays a crucial role in overall teaching quality because it addresses the actions teachers must take to create an environment that supports and facilities both academic and social emotional learning (e.g., Evertson and Weinstein, 2006). Since joining the Human Sciences International Degree program, most of my courses such as Human Rights, Global Citizenship, Anthropology and Contemporary Global Issues, Introduction to Civil Society Movements and Presentation Skills have received students from diverse geographical, cultural and linguistic backgrounds. The combination of different types of students (International Program students/ Japanese Students/ Exchange Students) has generated additional challenges for classroom management. Here I will address three major issues I observed in my courses.

Firstly, the level of English proficiency among the students is a major concern. Due to the language advantage, students who are L1 users of English are typically fast learners while L2 or L3 users of English may lack confidence in understanding course content and speaking English in the classroom. This is despite the fact that they have met the official English proficiency requirements for course enrolment. Most educators find it difficult to ensure the appropriate levels of English and course content are available to different types of students.

Secondly, cultural insensitivity between instructors and students, as well as among the students, can easily produce embarrassment, unintended insult, conflicts, tensions and some students feeling excluded. Taking my course Human Rights as an example, the course introduces the universal human rights principles to students; however this may clash with or contradict with the values of some students who have different belief systems, religions, moral values and cultural norms. If the teachers and students tend to take all knowledge and values for granted, some students may feel uncomfortable in expressing their views in the classroom. They may even lose interest in learning.

Thirdly, students come from varying cultural backgrounds; they also tend to have different learning styles (Ramburuth and McCormick, 2001). For example, studies show that there is no significant difference in approaches to learning and performance among students from different countries. However, American students tend to have a more social, interactive learning style, preferring to interact with peers and teachers, whilst Chinese students prefer to work with highly organized materials and lecture-based classes. The difference in learning styles could have implications on instruction methods and class management policies and practices. If you have students who are more used to an interactive and discussion-based learning environment, lecture-based teaching may not be the most effective method and vice versa. The kind of instruction methods the instructors use will have a direct impact on their students' engagement in learning. Therefore it is challenging for educators to find the appropriate teaching styles when the students are so diverse.

Some Suggestions for Managing the Multicultural Classroom

To overcome the above challenges, new classroom management strategies are necessary with particular attention being paid to attitudes and behaviour, course content and using a variety of teaching styles. Based on student evaluation and my classroom observation, these strategies have successfully created a positive learning atmosphere for students in my courses.

- **Building Respectful Attitudes in the Classroom**

Helping students recognize the importance of respect and tolerance is extremely important to manage multicultural classrooms. This works more effectively if the instructors can do it near the beginning of the course such as the first class. In my courses, I often explain to all students clearly the main objectives of the courses and invite them to work together to build a positive learning environment so that they can achieve the learning outcomes. For example, if class discussion is part of the learning process, it is important that students' comments and feedback should be on the basis of respect. Instead of merely focusing on hard knowledge, soft knowledge like interpersonal communication skills is equally important for student development. More studies are showing that the multicultural learning environment can prepare students to have better intercultural competence (more openness to cultural diversity, more globally minded) than those students studying in homogenous classrooms. Numerous studies also indicate that students having high intercultural competency can perform more effectively in a multicultural society and marketplace (e.g., Bennett, 1999; Deardorff, 2006; Soria and Troisi, 2014).

• **Making Course Content Relevant to Students**
Course content is also another key factor that influences students' learning

	Lecture Topics
	Part I Why Anthropology?
Week 1	Introduction
Week 2	Introduction: Anthropology and Globalization
Week 3	A Brief History of Anthropology I
Week 4	A Brief History of Anthropology II
Week 5	Traditional / Multi-sited Ethnography I
Week 6	Traditional / Multi-sited Ethnography II
Week 7	The Social Person & Society I
Week 8	The Social Person & Society II
	Part II The Engagement of Anthropology in Global Issues
Week 9	Health as Human Rights **AIDS in Africa**
Week 10	Economic Systems and Poverty I **Poverty in America**
Week 11	Economic Systems and Poverty II **Poverty in Bolivia**
Week 12	Gender, Culture and Development I **Gender Issues in Japan**
Week 13	Gender, Culture and Development II **Gender Issues relating to Muslim Women**
Week 14	Globalization I **Global Sushi**
Week 15	Globalization II / course wrap up

Table 10.1 *Anthropology and contemporary global issues.*

motivations. When the course content relates more to students' social experiences and cultural backgrounds, they are more likely to take the initiative for learning and participating in class discussion. For example, in my courses Anthropology and Contemporary Global Issues and Introduction to Civil Society Movements (see outlines provided in Tables 10.1 and 10.2), I have used examples from different countries that develop students' interest in the subjects and, more importantly, this allows students from diverse backgrounds to have an equal opportunity to share their opinions. The more active involvement of students in the learning process can help them to develop self-esteem and confidence as many studies have shown (e.g., Pianta, Hamre and Allen, 2012).

	Lecture Topics
	Part I Theoretical Approach to Civil Society
Week 1	Course Overview- What is Civil Society?
Week 2	Civil Society as Associational Life
Week 3	Civil Society as Good Society I
Week 4	Civil Society as Good Society II **Cases of China and Eastern European Countries**
Week 5	Civil Society as Public Sphere
Week 6	Civil Disobedience **(US, India, Turkey, HK, Taiwan)**
Week 7	What are Social Movements? I
Week 8	What are Society Movements? II
Week 9	Recap Concepts of Civil Society
	Part II Key Themes: Causes, Participation and Consequences
Week 10	Case 1 Japan **Tohoku and Voluntarism**
Week 11	Case 2 India **Pink Saris**
Week12	Case 3 **Chipko and World Rainforest Movement**
Week 13	Case 4 **Arab Spring**
Week 14	Review
Week 15	Conclusion So what's to be Done?

Table 10.2 *Introduction to civil society movements.*

- **Introducing Diverse Teaching Styles**

When dealing with students with different learning styles, educators can apply diverse teaching methods in the classes simultaneously. For example, in my course Anthropology and Contemporary Global Issues, I first give a brief lecture to introduce students to some key concepts in the lecture topic. After that, I often give students the worksheet (see the worksheet sample provided on the following page) so that they can have the opportunity to discuss what they have learnt during the lecture.

There are two parts in the worksheet: group discussion and individual written reflection. This mix of teaching styles (lecture— discussion— written reflection) works well with diverse students who have different learning preferences. Meanwhile, the worksheet can also help ESL students (English as second language students) to understand the course content easily and participate in the discussion. Studies show that diverse teaching styles and assignments not only fulfil different types of students' need but the approach allows educators to assess students' performance in a more comprehensive and fair way as we have mentioned in the previous section.

Part Two | Reflections on Teaching and Learning on an English-medium Program

Example of course worksheet

---

1 Anthropology and Contemporary Global Issues   Spring 2014

Class Discussion / Homework For <u>Week 3/4 Lecture What is Anthropology</u>

Student Name: _____

> Notice: Please **complete the Part III** and **the submission time will be announced in the class.** Class discussion and homework are parts of participation; no separate assessment will be given.

Part I: Class Discussion
Why do some of the practices and rituals of other cultures seem odd, strange or foreign to us? Share one example with your classmates and discuss how our own cultural norms affect our understanding and perception of other cultures.

Your example is _____

Part II: Film Screening and Discussion

Rabbit-Proof Fence (2002)
The film is based on a true story of Molly Craig, a young black Australian girl who leads her younger sister and cousin in an escape from an official government camp, set up as part of an official government policy to train them as domestic workers and integrate them into white society. Under the law in the 1930s, government officials had the right to seize **half-caste** children – those with both aborigine and white parentage- to be housed on native settlements, where they were to be **re-educated** to western ways eventually to become servants for whites. With grit and determination Molly guides the girls on an epic journey, one step ahead of the authorities, over 1,500 miles of Australia's outback in search of the rabbit-proof fence that bisects the continent and will lead them home. These three girls are part of what is referred to today as part of the **Stolen Generations**.

1. What impression do you get of the role of the policeman in the community?
2. How do we know that the Aboriginal people fear the police?
3. Can you give me some examples of what sort s of words Mr. Neville, the Chief Protector of Aborigines use to justify taking away the girls?
4. How would you judge Neville? Can he seen as a product of his society?
5. What are the proposes of showing this film to you? How does this relates to the theme of lecture?

Anthropology and Contemporary Global Issues — Spring 2014

Part III

What is ethnocentrism? Do you think human beings almost everywhere are ethnocentric? What are some consequences of ethnocentrism? Use an example to illustrate your opinion.

References

Bennett, C. (1999). *Comprehensive multicultural education: Theory and practice (4th Ed)*. Boston: Allyn and Bacon.

Deardorff, D.K. (2006). Identification and assessment of intercultural competence as a student outcome of internationalization. *Journal of Studies in International Education, 10*(3), 241-266.

Evertson, C. M. and Weinstein, C. S. (Eds.) (2006). *Handbook of classroom management: Research, practice, and contemporary Issues.* London: Lawrence Erlbaum Associates.

Pianta, R. C., Hamre, B. K. and Allen, J. P. (2012). Teacher-student relationships and engagement: Conceptualizing, measuring, and improving the capacity of classroom interactions. In *Handbook of research on student engagement.* (pp. 365-386). Springer.

Ramburuth, P. and McCormick, J. (2001). Learning diversity in higher education: The comparative study of Asian international and Australian students. *Higher Education, 42,* 333-350.

Soria, K. M. and Troisi, J. (2014). Internationalization at home alternatives to study abroad: Implications for students' development of global, international, and intercultural competencies. *Journal of Studies in International Education, 18,* 261-280.

Eleven

Enhancing the Role of Teaching Assistants in the Delivery of English-medium Courses

Yukiko Ishikura

In this last section, I will talk about how to become an effective TA in English-medium courses and best maximize student learning. Over the past three years, I have been involved with the Human Sciences International Program courses as a senior TA and PhD student studying about English-medium programs and courses. I deeply feel that it requires time and effort for instructors and TAs to understand how to make the teaching and learning more effective and supportive with students from diverse backgrounds.

Introduction of TA System in Japanese Higher Education

In the late 1980s, the TA system was first implemented in Japanese national universities. However, it was only after 2000 that the TA system began to attract more attention as a result of the increasing demands of university reform, especially enhancing the quality of education (Kitano, 2005). The Central Council for Education (2011) declared the significance of adopting the TA system in Japanese universities and using the opportunities for graduate students to gain teaching experience as well as knowledge and skills to become future university instructors. It also noted that the presence of TAs in university education could enhance quality of education.

University education has been greatly impacted by increasing demands of enhancing TA systems and introducing English-medium courses. Since English-medium courses are characterized by student diversity, innovative course delivery and, of course, English is the medium of instruction, the TAs are required to possess different knowledge and skills compared to those assisting with regular Japanese courses.

Tips to Support Diverse Students in English-Medium Courses

In diverse teaching and learning environments, everyone (instructors, students and TAs) needs to be a learner. Here are some tips for TAs to assist students with diverse linguistic, cultural and learning backgrounds and expectations. The figure on the following page provides an overall picture of TA work, and I would like to raise some key points to assist students.

Understanding Students'/Instructors' Diversity and Different Ways of Learning/Teaching

English-medium courses attract a wide range of students with different linguistic, cultural and learning backgrounds and different expectations of teaching and learning. Students who are not L1 users of English are usually aware of linguistic challenges, but not of how their culture affects their learning. Academic cultures, academic disciplines and learning styles vary in different cultural contexts. We must understand that cultural differences and learning backgrounds can affect how students learn. This means that a single

When	How to support students
Before course	• Read the course syllabus to learn about the course objectives, learning outcomes, course contents and assignments • Meet an instructor to understand his/her expectations of the TA • Learn about students' diversity and their different ways of learning
First lecture	• Make sure to inform students of your presence and your role in the class • Spend 10 minutes providing tips to students who are unfamiliar with reading and writing in English
Before class	• Prepare the course materials and be familiar with them • Talk to your instructor and learn how the class will be delivered and how you can assist students and the instructor • Communicate with your students
In class	• Monitor student progress, achievements and behaviour • Support individual students • Make sure that group activities go smoothly and intervene if necessary
After class	• Communicate with your students and instructor verbally or through e-mail
Before assignment	• Clearly explain to students the assignment instructions and deadlines, both verbally and in writing • Tell students that you and the instructor are available for questions and concerns by e-mail or before/after class

Table 11.1 *Overview of the linguistic, cultural and learning support context for TAs.*

way of teaching and supporting does not suit all learners. We offer different kinds of support in response to different needs and expectations.

It is not only the students, but also the instructors in English-medium courses who have diverse linguistic, cultural and teaching backgrounds. Because of their various backgrounds, instructors also have different needs and expectations of TAs. TAs need to learn what instructors expect them to do and to develop teaching strategies with the instructor before the course begins.

Supporting Students Effectively and Appropriately in a Timely Manner

- **Your Presence and Role in Class**

In the first lecture, it is important for instructors and TAs to clearly inform students of the presence of the TAs and their role in the course. A clear explanation can help students contact TAs more easily.

- **When to Support**

Learning about how students learn and when they need support is vital. I used to only provide students with support when they sought it. However, my observations revealed that some students do not seek support even if they feel they need it. I also found that students tend to overestimate their learning capacity. These tendencies limit students' learning and what they can achieve. Students are not aware of how they are learning and how they can best maximize their learning. Instructors and TAs should be the ones in charge of the student learning. I also found that the beginning of the courses, the assessment periods and the end of the courses are times when students are the most overwhelmed and in need of support.

- **How to Support**

Creating Various Channels for Students to Access Instructors and TAs

- Communication with Instructors or TAs
- Before/In/After-Class Communication
- Verbal (Face-to-Face)/ Writing (E-mail) Communication

Students make different uses of time and space for their learning and communication. By creating a variety of channels through which students can access instructors and TAs, student progress, achievements and behaviour can be better monitored. Also, students should be made aware that both instructors and TAs are available to answer questions before, in or after class, or by e-mail.

TAs should be aware that students have different ways of establishing connections with instructors and TAs, as well as different ways and times of processing their learning. Some students feel more comfortable talking to instructors while others prefer talking to TAs. Also, some prefer direct face-to-face communication and others prefer indirect communication, such as e-mail. Some prefer in-class communication and others prefer before or after-class communication. Furthermore some require a longer time to process all the information they receive in class than others.

Important announcements, such as assignment directions or deadlines, have been the concerns and questions students have asked me the most. For such announcements, I make sure that I send an e-mail notification to everyone, with supplements in Japanese translation for very important information. At the end of each e-mail message, I add that both instructors and TAs are available to answer their questions or concerns by e-mail or in class. It is just a small thing, but it can make a big difference. After such e-mails, I quite often receive questions by e-mail or after class.

When talking to students and trying to understand their concerns, TAs need to make sure they inform instructors of what students say, and vice versa. Talking with instructors about student learning concerns and progress can provide them with a better idea of how to enhance student teaching and learning.

- **Assisting Students to Be Familiar with Different Academic Work**

As I mentioned earlier, academic disciplines vary from country to country. Students, therefore, have different academic skills. In the English-medium courses that constitute the International Program, some students will face challenges concerning the academic work: for example reading, writing and discussions. Japanese mainstream program students, the majority of those taking the non-G30 courses, are often overwhelmed by all of the unfamiliar course work in English.

1) Reading and Writing

Universities in some countries do not require much reading and writing for the courses. Hence, some students are surprised to see how much reading and writing are required to complete the courses. If these students are not L1 users of English, the first couple of weeks can be very challenging period of time for them. Some students told me that they spent the entire week translating every single word of the assigned reading into their own language. Learning how to skim and summarize the important points in the texts are skills that students need to develop to survive the semester.

As for writing, it is important for TAs to ensure that students 'critically argue their opinions' and cite and reference appropriately. Those are the skills students are required to have in the International Program courses. Some students do not know how to critically argue their opinions in their writing assignments. Often, I have seen students summarizing their reading without voicing their own opinions. Some academic cultures require you to critically read and argue your statements with cited sources to support your opinions, and some value agreeing with the instructors or the authors of the texts (e.g., McLean and Ransom, 2005, p. 54). It is also important to make sure that students cite/reference sources they have used to support their critical arguments. Sample writings or citation/reference guidelines would be helpful for students.

If possible, I would suggest spending some time early on in the course covering the following reading and writing tips for those students who are unfamiliar with reading and writing:

- How to skim and summarize the key points of the reading assignments
- How to read and write critically (explain what 'critically argue' means)
- How to cite and reference appropriately

2) Discussion

Discussions can be the most challenging task for some students since they involve language, culture and academic skills. Japanese students, for example, are often unfamiliar with the language used in class and discussions. In addition, their cultural nature or their sensitive guessing ability hinders them from actively participating in these activities. Japanese students employ sensitive guessing ability, or *Sasshi*, as a way to behave in socially appropriate ways depending on the context, taking into consideration factors like place (*ba*) and space or timing (*ma*) to create and preserve harmony (*wa*) (Yamashita, 2012, p. 37).

TAs can become more aware of the language, culture and academic skills involved with the challenges of discussions; however, discussions are also appropriate occasions for students to learn how to be respectful of other cultures and different ways of learning.

English-medium courses in Japan provide instructors, students and TAs with learning opportunities in more international settings. For a TA in particular, it is a significant opportunity to pose questions about what learning and teaching actually are and to examine how to provide the best support in international and intercultural classrooms. I strongly believe that the presence of a TA in class and his/her effective appropriate support can make a big difference to student teaching and learning processes and outcomes. I hope this chapter can help you to better support students and enjoy being a part of the student learning process.

References

Central Council for Education (2011). *Graduate school education for globalized society: Graduate students to be successful in multiple discipline in the world* [global ka shakai no daigakuin kyoiku: sekai no tayo na bunya de daigakuin shuryosha ga katsuyaku surutameni] http://www.mext.go.jp/component/b_menu/shingi/toushin/_icsFiles/afieldfile/2011/03/04/1301932_01.pdf.

Kitano, A. (2005). Trends on research of teaching assistants in Japan [wagakuni no teaching assistant seido kenkyu no doko]. *Nihon University Society for Educational Research, 40*, 49-61.

McLean, P. and Ransom, L. (2005). Building intercultural competencies: implications for academic skills development. In J. Carroll and J. Ryan (Eds.), *Teaching international students: improving learning for all*. Oxen: Routledge.

Yamashita, M. (2012). The experience of Japanese graduate students in U.S. higher education: An investigation of the challenges they face in the classroom. *Reitaku Journal of Interdisciplinary Studies, 20*(2), 27-42.

Part Three

– From Handbook to Practice

Beverley A. Yamamoto
Don Bysouth

Twelve

Conclusion
– Enhancing Quality and Practice

Beverley A. Yamamoto and Don Bysouth

This Handbook has provided some brief guidelines and suggestions for best practice with regard to what we take to be the most important elements involved with the teaching and delivery of undergraduate level courses. Those elements include curriculum development, instructional methods, assessment strategies, moderation procedures and feedback practices. What we have attempted to stress is the importance of an approach to program design and delivery that promotes quality in teaching and learning by way of providing ways of building a 'quality scaffolding'. In other words, by promoting the adoption of a range of methods by which individual course designers might design courses that clearly promote learning of measurable skills, abilities and knowledge that relate to specific course objectives, and how such courses can be integrated to achieve program level outcomes. Of course, while we cannot hope to provide an all-inclusive handbook on teaching and learning for higher education, we hope that this Handbook may be of some utility in assisting with the design and implementation of high quality undergraduate level courses. Perhaps even more importantly, we hope that this Handbook may help guide and assist academic staff on key features of effective teaching practice that can be applied to the challenges of developing EMI programs in Japan and further afield.

Drawing on our experience working in a variety of higher education settings – and mindful of the challenges that come with working with often incommensurate pedagogical orientations, theories, and practices – we have attempted to adopt a pragmatic approach with this handbook. We have not drawn up a list of 'must dos', a definitive list of what you should do to successfully plan and implement an EMI program. Instead, we have attempted to outline some effective scaffolding strategies with clear, practical examples drawn from our own endeavours to document and implement a range of teaching and learning practices for use in a new undergraduate degree program – notably one that has been implemented and delivered within a challenging range of cultural and organizational constraints.

It is worthwhile stressing again that high quality teaching does *not* simply arise by virtue of having experienced educators, bright and capable students, and a wealth of institutional resources. Instead, it requires that care and attention be directed towards ensuring that there is alignment between clear course and program learning outcomes, course delivery mechanisms, assessment practices, feedback systems, and a commitment to on-going program development. Perhaps as a start, individual course designers and instructors might be better able to provide answers to such straightforward questions as '*what do I want my students to learn in my course*' and '*how can I accurately measure if my students have learned what my course is designed to teach*' when this takes place in settings in which the higher level objectives are given (at least) some credibility.

In our experience there are a number of barriers to creating and implementing high quality courses and programs that are of particular relevance to educators undertaking internationalization initiatives from within more traditional systems. Some of these might best be conveyed by the following statements, which represent a collection of the kinds of anecdotal and informal opinions we have received in our quality enhancement endeavours:

> '*This is how I have run my course for years – why should I have to change?*'

> '*This is how the system works here – why should we have to change?*'

> '*I do not have time to spend on developing my courses due to many other commitments.*'

> '*Some professors are naturally good at using particular teaching methods but I am not.*'

> '*In my discipline we do not use those kinds of teaching methods or assessments – why should I consider how other disciplines do these things?*'

> '*Why should I provide reports or other documentation about my courses to other professors or administrators?*'

'My professors did it this way, so if it was good enough for them it is good enough for my students.'

'I do not want my performance as a professor or teacher evaluated.'

Rather than focus on any of these questions specifically, perhaps one way of broadly dealing with such challenges is to consider that the increasing focus on external delivery of higher education via the use of information and communication technologies (ICT), with computer-supported collaborative learning (CSCL), massively open online course (MOOCs), and collaborative online international learning (COIL), *requires* higher education professionals to adapt to changes in global perceptions of what constitutes good educational delivery and practice. Moreover, universities face increasing competition for students and must provide clear and demonstrable evidence that they are providing educational services that are of high quality and utility.

With regard to cultural challenges faced when developing and implementing English medium programs in universities that are non-English speaking, it is important to note that scholars have argued that internationalisation policies in Asia often fail to adequately provide for detailed, critical reflection on the implications of utilising English with regard to the preservation and further development of indigenous cultural capital (e.g., Phan Le Ha, 2013). Other scholars have highlighted the growth in EMI courses and programs (particularly in the Asian region) as being predominantly the result of government initiatives to attract international students, ostensibly to raise university rankings on international ranking tables and to raise additional revenue to support domestic student enrolments (e.g., Kirkpatrick, 2014). However, our position is that arguments such as the former often radically overstate the negative impacts of English with regard to EMI or English as lingua franca (e.g., Ikeda and Bysouth, 2013) and often fail to consider the impact of organizational change occurring within the higher education sector throughout the developed world. We can remember very similar statements of resistance as those mentioned above when the first effects of the Bologna alignment policies started to be felt in the UK. In addition, they may fail to adequately assess the benefits that may accrue with the implementation of EMI courses and programs within universities that seek greater scholarly and cultural exchange within an increasingly globalized higher education sector.

In this regard, and mindful of cultural, linguistic and organizational challenges, with increasing globalization a significant premium is attached to the transferability of knowledge and skills across national borders, there is a growing need to ensure that universities ensure that administrative and institutional accounting (e.g., course credits, grades) can be credibly and reliably provided. Increasingly, students are unlikely to select universities simply on the basis of reputation or prestige alone, particularly when they can easily determine the quality of individual courses by way of interacting with current and former students using social media. The allure of study abroad and exchange programs may be greatly diminished when inbound students find they are enrolled in courses that are ill-defined in terms of learning outcomes, assessment strategies, and related areas. More pragmatically, students may find they cannot transfer course credits to their home institutions as the result of failure by a host institution to ensure high quality in course and program delivery.

Regardless of the language used in instruction, it is important to consider how best to manage these concerns in ways that promote good teaching practice. Stripped down to basics, our approach is to highlight the importance of developing learning outcomes for individual courses, levels and in turn entire programs of study, and the use of criteria based grading that links assessment with learning outcomes at any particular level of a program. This is not to create undue burdens on academic or administrative staff, but to specify with some degree of precision what is being taught, how it is being taught, how learning is assessed, and to provide frameworks by which teaching and learning can be subject to continuing quality enhancement. Moreover, while some readers may argue that employing a constructive alignment approach to outcomes based teaching and learning, such as the one we have adopted from Briggs and Tang (2007), 'might sound difficult, time consuming and way too idealistic. That is not what an increasingly large number of university teachers are finding' (p. 7). We would certainly be happy to be counted amongst those educators that find such an approach, not idealistic or needlessly difficult, but of great utility in helping improve our individual teaching practices and more broadly for the improvement of our program as a whole.

References

Biggs, J. and Tang, C. (2007). *Teaching for quality learning at university (3rd Ed.)*. Maidenhead: Open University Press/McGraw Hill.

Ikeda, K. and Bysouth, D. (2013). Japanese and English as lingua francas: Language choices for international students in contemporary Japan. In H. Haberland, D. Lønsmann, and B. Preisler (Eds.), *Language Alternation, Language Choice and Language Encounter in International Tertiary Education*. Springer Publishers.

Kirkpatrick, A. (2014). English as a medium of instruction in East and Southeast Asian Universities. In N. Murray and A. Scarino (Eds.), *Dynamic ecologies: A relational perspective on languages education in the Asia-Pacific region*. Springer.

Phan Le Ha. (2013). Issues surrounding English, the internationalization of higher education and national cultural identity in Asia: a focus on Japan. *Critical Studies in Education, 54*(2), 160-175.